LATIN FOR ALTAR BOYS

An Easy Introduction to the
Latin Words in the Mass for
Boys Who Serve at the Altar

by

Hugh Ballantyne

Copyright 2011

Dedicated to

Aedan

because he gets up early in the morning to serve Mass, as I did many years ago, and because he took time out from important things like hockey to help me with this book.

Index

Preface	6
Lesson 1 A bit about English: Three new words	8
Lesson 2 A bit about Latin: "Tail-changing"	13
Lesson 3 The Sign of the Cross	18
Lesson 4 Patris et Filii	23
Lesson 5 Et Spiritus Sancti	26
Lesson 6 More About English	33
Lesson 7 Introibo	37
Lesson 8 Tense	42
Lesson 9 The Accusative Case	47
Lesson 10 Qui laetificat juventutem meam	53

Lesson 11 Judica me Deus	57
Lesson 12 De gente non sancta	63
Lesson 13 Quia tu es Deus	69
Lesson 14 Emitte lucem tuam	77
Lesson 15 Confitebor	83
Lesson 16 Spera in Deo	90
Lesson 17 Gloria Patri	94
Lesson 18 The *Confiteor*	99
Lesson 19 Misereatur	106
Lesson 20 Indulgentiam	114

Lesson 21 Deus tu conversus	120
Lesson 22 Nearly Finished	125
Lesson 23 Suscipiat Dominus	131
Lesson 24 This can't be right!	137
Lesson 25 Pater noster	139
Lesson 26 Communion	142
Lesson 27 Blessing	147
Answers	148
My Latin Vocabulary	158

Preface

This book has three objectives.

The first objective is to enable boys, who serve the old Mass, to understand the Latin words which they speak and hear during Mass. Longer parts of the Mass, like the Credo or the Canon, where the server is silent, are not included. And there is nothing about Latin pronunciation here. You must learn how to *say* the words, when you learn how to serve Mass. And you have to learn how to serve Mass BEFORE you can use this book.

The second objective is to provide a pre-Latin course. When a boy, who serves Mass, goes on later to study Latin in high school or college, this book should give him a head-start.

A final objective is to provide the young person with a grounding for the study of any language, including English. With that in mind, we try to present—in a simplified way—both the relevant concepts of classical grammar, and some of the insights of modern linguistic theory.

Is this book only for boys? By no means. However, the book does presume that you are familiar with—and know how to pronounce—the words of the Latin Mass. It should appeal equally, therefore, to any family member who is already accustomed to making the responses during a dialogue Mass in the old rite.

How should I use this book? Please, do not simply hand this book to your son and tell him to read it. Sit down and read it with him. Invite him to read it <u>out loud</u>. When questions come up, discuss them. Do not proceed too quickly. If the child is under 12, slow down and give more help.

If you love serving Mass, and if you would like to understand the Latin words that you hear and say at Mass, then this book is for you! This book requires almost no memorization. It is not a Latin textbook. As you work your way through the lessons, you will start to remember what the Latin words mean without any difficulty. There are exercises at the end of each lesson. They are there to help you. They are not a test of your memory. If you do not know an answer, you are always allowed to turn back a few pages and look it up.

Lesson 1: <u>A Bit about English: 3 New Words</u>

1
     In order to start learning Latin, you first have to learn something about English.
     You already speak English, but you probably don't think about it very much. You just do it. From now on you will have to think about English and speak it at the same time. Try not to fall down.
     And by the way: It's a good idea to read this book out loud, even if you are alone.

2
     We are going to begin by learning three words. The words are:

     verb
     noun
     preposition

3

What is a *verb*?

A verb is an "action-word". For example:

     eat
     throw
     think

     When you are eating your vegetables, or throwing a football, you are *doing* something. You are performing an action.
     Even when you are quietly thinking about snakes, you are still *doing* something. The action is in your head. If somebody asks, "What are you doing", you can reply, "I'm thinking".

     So *eat, throw*, and *think* are action-words. They are verbs.

4

How can I tell for sure if a word is a verb?

A word is a verb, if you can put the word "we" in front of it to make a sentence. For example:

We eat.
We throw.
We think.

But "all" is not a verb, because you cannot just say "We all". If you insist on saying, "We all", folks will probably wait for you to finish your sentence. For example, "We all arrived on time".

5

What is a *noun*?

A noun is the name of a thing. A noun is what a thing is *called*.

For example, you probably possess a round object that you play with. That object is called a "ball".

And the word *ball* is a noun.

6

How can I tell for sure if a word is a noun?

A word is a noun, if you can fit it into the following sentence and make sense:

The .... is nice.

Is "ball" a noun? Yes, because you can fit it into that sentence and make sense:

The ball is nice.

Therefore "ball" must be a noun.

7

    Wait a minute! There's a problem here. I think the name "Henry" could be a noun. And the word "Texas" could also be a noun. But Henry and Texas are not *things*.

    Well..., now I'm not sure. I don't think Henry is a thing. Am I a thing? (You are welcome to answer that question, if you wish.)

    Anyway, we certainly can't say, "The Henry is nice". And we can't say, "The Texas is nice".

    So what gives?

8

    You are quite right. *Henry* and *Texas* are a special sort of noun. We call them "proper nouns", and they are always written with a capital letter.

9

    And now we have to upgrade our definition of "noun".

    What is a noun?

    A noun is the name of a person, place, or thing. A noun is what a person, place, or thing are called.

10

    Here is the third new word: *preposition*.

    The word *preposition* is hard to define. You can look it up in a dictionary if you like, but you won't be pleased with what you find.

11

    So instead of defining the word *preposition*, let's just compile a list of examples. I'll supply a few, and then you can add lots more.

I'm going to start with the odd phrase

.... the box

The space marked by four dots [....] stands for the words that we really want. For example

<u>in</u> the box
<u>under</u> the box
<u>near</u> the box.

The words *in*, *under*, and *near* are prepositions.

12

Now let's remove the box. Any noun will do.

in the future
under the impression
near the end

The words *in*, *under*, and *near* are still prepositions. Can you supply some more examples? Five would be nice.

13

Did you say, "On top of the box"?
It's a good answer. It's an excellent answer. But we want one-word answers here. And "on top of" is three words.

14

I once had a smarty-pants student who said, "What about *eat the box, smash the box, throw the box*? Are those words prepositions too."

No, they are not. They are verbs. Verbs have an altogether different social life from prepositions. Meanwhile, just notice this distinction:

When you say, "Throw the box", you are giving an order. Most of us will understand what you want us to do.

When you say, "In the box", you could be answering a question. For example:
"Where is the ball?"
"In the box."

But if you are not answering a question, and you just say the words "in the box" in the middle of nowhere, most of us will be puzzled. We will not know what you want to tell us.

15

What have we learned so far?

We have learned the words *noun*, *verb*, and *preposition*.
We have learned a definition of *noun*, and a definition of *verb*. But we did not learn a definition of *preposition*. Instead, we made a list of prepositions.
We learned methods for identifying whether a particular word is a noun, a verb, or a preposition.

16

Review Questions:

What is a *noun*?
    Give three examples.

What is a *proper noun*?
    Give three examples.

What is a *verb*?
    Give three examples.

What is a *preposition*?
    Give three examples.

PS: If you are not sure, ask for help. Grown-ups know this stuff pretty well.

Lesson 2: A Bit about Latin: "Tail-Changing"

1

    Have you noticed something when you are serving Mass?

    At the beginning of the Mass the priest says:

       In nomine Patris et Filii et Spiritus Sancti

    The words that we are interested in here are

       > *Patris et Filii et Spiritus Sancti*

    Perhaps you already know what those words mean. If you do, fine. If you don't, don't worry.

2

    Toward the end of the Mass the priest says:

       Benedicat vos omnipotens Deus,
          Pater et Filius et Spiritus Sanctus.

    The words we are interested in this time are

       > *Pater et Filius et Spiritus Sanctus*

3

    Same or different?   First we had

       <u>Patris et Filii et Spiritus Sancti</u>

and then we had

       <u>Pater et Filius et Spiritus Sanctus</u>

Same or different?

Oops! They are not exactly the same. What's going on here?

4   Latin words have <u>different forms</u>. They "shape-shift". They morph into something else. They change their endings, the way a lizard changes its tail.

For example we have:

Pater and *Patris*, and they both mean "father"

Filius and *Filii*, and they both mean "son"

Sancti and *Sanctus*, and they both mean "holy".

We also saw:

Spiritus the first time, and then *Spiritus* again the second time. Those two appear to be the same. But, as we shall see later, there is an invisible difference between them.

5   English words also change their form. For example we say:

sing, sang, sung, song, songs, sings, singer, and *singing*

One little base-word seems to have 8 different forms. The Chinese consider that this sort of thing makes English a difficult language. But boys who speak English do not find it difficult at all.

6   English has lots of prepositions. Latin also has lots of prepositions.

English words can "shape-shift", or change their form. Latin words also "shape-shift" and change their form.

So what's the big difference between the two languages?

The difference is that English uses prepositions MORE than Latin does. And Latin uses form-changing A LOT MORE than English does.

7

Now we mentioned that there was an invisible difference between the word *Spiritus* in section 1 and the word *Spiritus* in section 2 of this Lesson. (Look back at page 13 if you like: the words are in different boxes.)

You might ask, "If the difference is invisible, then why should I care about it?"

Quite right. If the topic does not interest you, then skip it and go on to Lesson 3. You do not need to know this.

8

However, if the topic does interest you, then here is the explanation. (Before reading it, please try to forget anything that you learned about long and short vowels in school.)

In Latin there are five vowels: a, e, i, o, u. You already know how to pronounce them. They are called "short vowels", because they only take about ¼ of a second to pronounce or say.

There are also five long vowels in Latin. During the time of the ancient Romans the long vowels were exactly the same as the short vowels, except that they took twice as long to say.

The long vowels can be written with a bar over them, like this: ā, ē, ī, ō, ū. However, many books, including ALL missals, omit the bar. They do not print it. The ancient Romans never bothered to write the bar at all. Furthermore, in the modern pronunciation of Latin everybody now pronounces the long vowels exactly the same as the short vowels. In fact, long vowels disappeared from spoken Latin about 500 AD. So it's been a while.

In this book the bar over a long vowel will be written when it is useful. And for the rest of the time it will be omitted.

9

We are now in a position explain the invisible difference between *spiritus* and *spiritus*. You have probably already guessed it.

Spiritus sanctus means   "Holy Spirit"

Spiritūs sancti means   "of the Holy Spirit"

So you see, this is a case where English uses the preposition "of", and Latin uses a tiny change of word-form to do the same job.

10

i. Review questions:

What is an important difference between English and Latin?

What is another form of *pater*?
What is another form of *filius*?
What is another form of *sanctus*?

ii. Hard review question:

If *Spiritūs* (with a bar) means "of the Spirit", what do *patris* and *filii* mean? Even if you don't feel sure, take a guess.

11
Preview

We are now ready to look at the actual words of the Mass. We have learned a little bit about English; and we have learned a little bit about Latin. From now on, we are going to jump in and "start swimming".

As we advance, we will also do some more grammar. Grammar is your friend. It is there to help you. Please do not think of it as a chore or a burden. The purpose of grammar is to help you understand more easily.

If hockey did not have rules, we could not play the game. If language did not have rules, we could not talk to each other. The rules of the game of language are called *grammar*.

A Note about Accent Marks

In any word—whether in English or in Latin—one syllable will always be louder than the other syllables of the same word. Say *Colorado* out loud. The syllable *ra* should be louder than the other syllables.

The loud syllable in a word is said to be "accented". If you have any trouble accenting the right syllable in Latin, look in your Missal. In the Missal, when a word has three or more syllables, an accent-mark will be printed over the loud syllable.

For example: confíteor is different from confitébor.

You are welcome to make notes in this book. And if you find it helpful to add accent marks, go right ahead. Best of all, get the sound in your head by saying the words out loud.

Lesson 3: <u>The Sign of the Cross</u>

1

In nomine Patris et Filii et Spiritūs sancti, Amen.

Let's begin with *in nomine*. It means, "in the name".

Is something missing?

2

The word for "the" is missing. There is no word for "the" in Latin. There is also no word for "a" or "an" in Latin.
So *in nomine* can mean "in name", or "in <u>a</u> name", or "in <u>the</u> name".
We'll stay with "in <u>the</u> name", because that seems to sound best in English.

3

We're not quite finished with *in nomine* yet.

If you look "name" up in an English-Latin dictionary, it will give you *nomen*. Not *nomine*.
So what's going on here?

4

The Latin word for "name" has (at least) two different forms.

There is the dictionary-form, *nomen*.
And there is the form for use after the preposition "in", which is *nomine*. For the time being let's call that the "after *in* form".

Dictionary form: *nomen*
After-*in* form: *nomine*

And they mean EXACTLY the same thing: "name".

And if this seems a bit messy and repetitive, that's because it is. All human languages—including English—are messy and repetitive.

5

    The different forms of a Latin noun are called "cases".

    The dictionary-form is called the "nominative case".

    The after-*in* form is called the "ablative case".

    There is no need for you to memorise those terms. We are going to use them so often, that you will remember them whether you want to or not.

    Nomen is in the nominative case.
    Nomine is in the ablative case.

    And they both mean "name".

6

    What is the nominative case used for? That's a secret. We'll talk about it some other time.

    The ablative case is used after the preposition *in*.

    We have now finished with *in nomine*. Do you remember what it means?

7

    In nomine Patris

    Take a guess at what those words mean. (You've just been given some instructions. So please STOP reading, and obey the instructions!)

    Did you guess, "in the name of the Father"? You were right! How come you already know Latin?

    And remember: there is no word for "the" in Latin.

8

    So *patris* means "of the Father".

    The dictionary form of this word is *pater*. Another (and more official) way of saying that is: "The nominative case of this word is *pater*".

    We could call *patris* the "of-form". The official name of this form is the "genitive case". You may call it the "of-form" or you may call it the "genitive case".
    It is used when you want to say, "of".

9

    Pater is the dictionary form of *patris*. *Patris* is the of-form of *pater*.
    Pater is in the nominative case. *Patris* is in the genitive case.

10

    We do the same thing in English. Look at these two sentences:

    Aedan is here.
    Aedan's ball is in the box.

    Nominative case: *Aedan*
    Genitive case: *Aedan's*

11

    You might object: But we spell *Aedan's* with an apostrophe (which is what that little doohickey is called).
    Quite true. But nobody HEARS the apostrophe. What we hear is the [z] sound after the name *Aedan*.

12 <u>Let's review the meanings</u>:

In nomine Patris means *In the name of the Father*

In means *In*

nomine means *the name*

patris means *of the Father.*

13 <u>Now let's review the grammar.</u>

In is a preposition. *Nomen* and *pater* are nouns.

Nomine is the "after-*in*" case. The correct name for that is the "ablative case". We use the ablative case after the preposition *in*.
Nomine is in the ablative case.

The dictionary form of this word is *nomen*. *Nomen* is in the nominative case.

The nominative of *patris* is *pater*. The genitive of *pater* is *patris*.

Patris is the "of-form", or the genitive case. We use the genitive case when we want to say "of".

14 Review questions:

 What do we mean by "case"?

 When do we use the ablative case?

 When do we use the genitive case?

 Does the English language have any different cases?

This is not a test of memory. If you have forgotten the answer to any of these questions, just turn back a page or two and find it. And make a written note or a mark on the page too, if that will help you.

15 Preview questions for the next lesson:

 What does *Filii* mean? What case is *Filii*?

 What does *Spiritūs sancti* mean? What case is *Spiritūs sancti* ?

 What does *et* mean?

See if you can guess the right answers without turning the page.

Lesson 4: Patris et Filii

1

In nomine Patris et Filii et Spiritūs sancti. Amen

    In the name of the Father
    and of the Son
    and of the Holy Spirit. Amen

2

Perhaps you don't care to repeat the word "of". Perfectly acceptable. Leave it out after the first time.

    In the name of the Father
    and [...] the Son
    and [...] the Holy Spirit.

Thus we can either say "of" three times, or else we can understand "of" without repeating it. Both options are correct, and, it makes no difference in Latin.

3

Filii means "of the Son". *Filii* is the "of-form". *Filii* is in the genitive case.

Here are three ways to ask one and the same question:

a) What is *filii* the "of-form" of?   (Better say that out loud!)
    b) What is the dictionary form of *filii* ?
    c) What is the nominative case of *filii* ?

And the answer to all three questions is the same:

Filius

4

Filius is in the nominative case, and it means "the son". *Filii* is in the genitive case, and it means "of the son".

Remember that in section 6 of Lesson 2 we decided that we do not know what the nominative case is used for. We still don't know. It's a secret.

5

This book is too long! We haven't even finished the Sign of the Cross yet, and we're already on page 23. Do I have to memorise all this stuff?

Relax. In this book you do not have to memorise anything. The book may seem long for two reasons. First, the pages are designed with plenty of room so that you can make your own notes on them. And second, there is a LOT of repetition at the beginning. We say the same thing in a lot of different ways. We will speed up as we advance.

6

So how should I use this book?

You should read through the whole text slowly, preferably out loud. <u>And you should be sure that you understand everything</u>. If there is something that you do not understand, ask for help.

The main goal of this book is to help you understand the Latin words, as you speak and hear them at Mass.

You can test your own success. Take some Latin words from the Mass, that you have already studied in this book. Translate them out loud slowly for somebody else. If you can do that, then you have succeeded. You have achieved the main purpose of this book.

In nomine Patris et Filii

If you know what exactly those five words mean, then you have completed the fourth lesson.

Review Exercises

What is the dictionary form of *nomine*?

What is the dictionary form of *Patris*?

What is the dictionary form of *Filii*?

Translate these English words into Latin:

In the name of the Father and of the Son

Lesson 5: Et Spiritus sancti

1

Spiritūs sancti means "of the Holy Spirit".

Latin can also say *sancti Spiritūs,* using the opposite word order.

Spiritūs sancti and *sancti Spiritūs* mean the same thing in Latin.

But in English we do not say "spirit holy".

Latin is more flexible about word-order.

2

Now we have a problem. *Spiritus sancti* is two words. And thus far we have only worked with one Latin word at a time.

So we must introduce a new grammatical term. The new term is

adjective.

Do you remember the three new words from Lesson 1? They were

    verb
    noun
    preposition.

Now we have four:

    verb
    noun
    preposition
    adjective

3

What is an adjective?

An adjective is a word that goes with a noun. And the adjective tells you what sort of noun you have.

Oh dear! That sounds very unhelpful. So let's talk about balloons.

4

Imagine that I am a balloon dealer. I sell balloons. You come to me, and you hold out some money. And I say, "Which balloon do you want?".

You can reply, "The red balloon", or "the big balloon", or "the small balloon", or even "the big, fat, ugly balloon". (The last answer is nice. But, as before, we want a one-word answer.)

The different words in your answer are all ADJECTIVES. The words

red
big
small
fat, and
ugly

are all adjectives. They go with the word "balloon". They tell me what sort of balloon you want.

And that is why we said, " An adjective is a word that goes with a noun. And the adjective tells you what sort of noun you have".

Grammarians say that an adjective MODIFIES the noun. They say that the adjective *red* modifies the noun *balloon*.

But if you want to go on saying, "The adjective *red* goes with the noun *balloon*.", that will be perfectly acceptable.

5

How can I tell for sure whether a word is an adjective or not?

Here is the method. Take any noun, for example

BOY.

Put the word "the" in front of it.

THE BOY.

Then put a space between them. The space should only be big enough for one word to fit in.

THE....BOY.

Any word that can fit into that space and make sense will have to be an adjective. For example,

> the big boy
> the small boy
> the good boy
> the bad boy.

Any word, that can fit between the word "the" and a following noun, has to be an adjective. Say that out loud.

6

When a noun and an adjective come together, they are called a

NOUN PHRASE

"The big boy" is not a noun. It is three words. It is a noun-phrase.

7

Spiritus sancti is also a noun-phrase. (Remember that there is no word for "the" in Latin.)

Spiritūs is a noun in the genitive case.

Sancti is an adjective in the genitive case.

Spiritus sancti means "of the Holy Spirit".

8

Wait a minute! How can they both be in the genitive case, if they have different ENDINGS? *Spiritūs* ends in –ūs, and *sancti* ends in –i.
Excellent question! Put it on hold. We'll come back to it in section 12 of this lesson.

9

Here is a rule:

<u>When you have a noun-phrase in Latin, the adjective has to be in the same case as the noun.</u>

So if the noun is genitive, the adjective has to be genitive. If the noun is in the ablative case, the adjective has to be in the ablative case. If the noun is in the nominative case, the adjective has to be in the nominative case.

If an adjective <u>goes with</u> a noun, the adjective and the noun have to be in the same case.

10

So *Spiritūs sancti* is a noun-phrase in the genitive case.

Both words are in the genitive case.

Sancti is an adjective, and *Spiritūs* is a noun, and *sancti* modifies *Spiritūs*.

And *Spiritūs sancti* means *of the Holy Spirit.*

11

Amen is a Hebrew word. It never changes.

12

One big question remains. In section 8 we asked: How can the noun *spiritūs* and the adjective *sancti* both be in the genitive case, if they have different endings?

Spiritūs ends in *–ūs,* and *sancti* ends in *–i* . So how come they are both in the of-form, or the genitive case?

13

Here is a guess: Nouns form the genitive case in one way, and adjectives form the genitive case in a different way.

Wait a minute! That can't be right. *Patris* and *filii* are both nouns, and they are both in the genitive case, and they have different endings. *Patris* ends in *–is,* and *filii* ends in *–i* . And they are both in the of-form, or the genitive case.

What is going on here?

14

Actually adjectives and nouns form the genitive case in exactly the same way as each other.

But there are five different ways to form the genitive case in Latin. That is, there are five different patterns.

These different patterns, or "case-families", are called *declensions*. A declension is a pattern for forming case-endings.

15

For nouns and adjectives there are 5 declensions in Latin.

We have not yet seen an example from the first declension.

Filius and *sanctus* are in the second declension. So they form the genitive case in the same way. Or—if you prefer—they make the of-form in the same way. The genitive case of *filius* is *filii*, and the genitive case of *sanctus* is *sancti*.

They both end in *–i*

16

    The part of the word that never changes is called the *stem*.

    The stem of *filii* is <u>*fili*–</u>. And the stem of *sancti* is <u>*sanct*–</u>.

    And the genitive ending of both of them is exactly the same: *–i*.

    So you might say that the ending "–i " means "of". And, in the second declension, you would be right.

17

    The word *pater* is in the <u>third</u> declension.

    The of-form, or genitive case, of *pater* is *patris*.

    The dictionary form, or nominative case, is *pater*. The stem is *patr-* , and the genitive ending is *–is*. So if we put a hyphen between the stem and the ending, it will look like this

        patr-is

    And that means *of the father*.

18

    We will talk about the other declensions when we come to them.

Review Exercises

A. What is the nominative case—or dictionary form—of *Patris*?

What is the nominative case of *Filii*?

Translate *of the Holy Spirit* into Latin.

B. The next exercise is more difficult. You have to compose Latin phrases that you have never seen before. You can do it!

Translate into Latin:

Holy Father
Holy Son
of the holy Son
of the holy Father

Lesson 6: <u>More About English</u>

1

    Do you remember the three new words?   They were

        verb
        noun
        preposition.

    Then we added one more, and there were four:

        verb
        noun
        preposition
        adjective.

    And now we have to add another one. The newest new word is

        pronoun.

    So now there are five:

        verb
        noun
        preposition
        adjective
        pronoun.

2

    What is a pronoun?

    A pronoun is a word like *I, me, you, he, she, it, we* or *they*. Of course, there are others. But those are some of the more important ones.

    It is difficult to define the word "pronoun". So we shall not bother trying.

However, it is easy to recognise pronouns. They jump around. Pronouns change their meanings.

3

Pronouns have a peculiar feature. They refuse to stand still. They change their meanings all the time.

For example, if I am talking about your mother and I say "she", then the pronoun *she* refers to your mother. But if I am talking about your sister, and I say "she", then exactly the same pronoun *she* refers to your sister.

Red always means "red". *Boy* always means "boy". But words like *she* can jump around.

If you are speaking, and you say, "me", you mean you. And if you are speaking to me and you say "you", you mean me. Or something like that. Pronouns get mixed up.

If you are talking about your family, and you say "they", that means the other members of your family. But if you are talking about your hockey team, and you say "they", then exactly the same word means the other members of your hockey team.

Pronouns are slippery.

4

A pronoun can almost always be replaced by a noun-phrase or a noun.

For example, the pronoun *they* might be replaced by the noun-phrase *the kids on my hockey team*. You can say, "<u>The kids on my hockey team</u> are really good skaters", or you can say, "<u>They</u> are really good skaters."

The pronoun *she* might be replaced by the noun *Granny*.
 "<u>She</u> is here" = "<u>Granny</u> is here."   It all depends.

That's what the word *pronoun* means. *Pronoun* means *instead of a noun*.

5

A few pronouns are hard to replace. It would be hard to find a noun to use in place of the pronouns *I* or *you*.

Try to find a different way of saying "I". Let me know if you succeed.

6

Why do we have to talk about pronouns in this book?

We have to understand pronouns in order to understand **verbs**. And verbs are in the next lesson. And verbs are the most important words in any language.

7

Pronouns are like socks in a drawer. If you don't keep them well organised, you will have trouble finding the ones you want.

Pronouns are organised in two ways. The first way is "singular" versus "plural".

Here are some singular pronouns. They only refer to one person or thing: *I, he, she, it*.

Here are some plural pronouns. They can refer to lots of people or things: *we, they*.

The pronoun *you* is both singular and plural in modern English. In old-fashioned English, however, *you* was only plural. The singular was *thou*. Where have I heard that before? Hint: think of the *Hail Mary*. We will sometimes include *thou* in this book, because Catholic altar-boys are often familiar with it.

8

Pronouns are also organised by a feature called "person". Here is how that works:

I and *we* are called the first person. The pronoun *I* is called the first person singular. And *we* is the first person plural.

Thou and *you* are called the second person. The pronoun *you* (or *thou*) is the second person singular. And *you* is also the second person plural.

He or *she* or *it* are the third person singular. And *they* is the third person plural.

9
Does that sound like a lot of stuff? Here is how to remember it:

I am first, and you are second, and everybody else is third.

Here is the same thing in the plural:

We are first, and you are second, and everything else is third.

This classification into *persons* (1st person, 2nd person, and 3rd person) will turn out to be very useful, when we look at verbs in the next lesson. And all grown-ups know it. And that is why you have to learn it

10
Here is a pronoun puzzle. It is make-believe. Suppose that you are playing soccer. Imagine that one of your team-mates doesn't speak English very well. After the game he says,

"Us were off-side, but the referee didn't see we".

You musn't laugh at him, because that would be rude. But what exactly was wrong with what he said?

Is it possible that English pronouns have different forms, or CASES, just like Latin?

PS: Did you answer those two question, or just read them and move on? What are the answers?

Lesson 7: <u>Introibo</u>

1

    Priest: Introibo ad altare Dei.
    Server: Ad Deum qui laetificat juventutem meam.

2

    <u>Introibo</u> means "I shall go in". <u>Introibo</u> is a verb.

3

    Now we had better pause here, and take another short look at verbs. Let's begin by reviewing what we learned in Lesson 1.

    What is a *verb*?

    A verb is an "action-word". For example:

        eat
        throw
        think

    When you are eating your vegetables, or throwing a football, you are *doing* something. You are performing an action.
    Even when you are quietly thinking about snakes, you are still *doing* something. The action is in your head. If somebody asks, "What are you doing?", you can reply, "I'm thinking".

    So *eat, throw*, and *think* are action-words. They are verbs.

4

    How can I tell for sure if a word is a verb?

    A word is a verb, if you can put the word "we" in front of it to make a sentence. For example:

> We eat
> We throw
> We think

    But "all" is not a verb, because you cannot just say "We all". If you insist on saying, "We all", folks will probably wait for you to finish your sentence. For example, "We all arrived on time".

5

    So <u>go</u> is definitely a verb. And <u>go in</u> is a verb-phrase. And <u>I shall go in</u> is an even longer verb-phrase.

6

    Now in the English language verbs are friendly with pronouns. Verbs and pronouns like to hold hands. In Latin, however, verbs and pronouns often avoid each other.

    The Latin word for "I" happens to be "ego".

    If you will look very hard at the words

> *Introibo ad altare Dei*,

you will notice something important about the Latin word *ego*. It is not there.

7

    Where did *ego* go?

    The answer is that the pronoun *ego* is bundled up inside the ending of the verb. You cannot see it.

    We use four English words, *I shall go in,* to translate one Latin word, *introibo*

    Now we need to take a grammatical knife, and we need to cut into the word *introibo*, in order to see what is packed inside it.

8

Intro- means "in", or "into".
You already knew that, because you know English words like "introspection", which means "looking inside yourself".

9

That leaves *–ibo*.
Does little *–ibo* all by itself mean "I shall go"? You bet.

-i- means "go". Yes! You heard right: -i- means "go".

And that leaves *–bo*.
–bo means "I shall".

In fact, we could cut even further, and split *–bo* up into two components. But it's hard to pronounce "b" by itself; so we'll stop there.

10

If you translate *introibo* into English with all the little bits lined up in the same order, you get

inside-go-shall-I.

But, of course, that's not the way we speak English.

11

In the last lesson we introduced pronouns. Well, here they are again.
Pronouns have NUMBER. That is, pronouns are either *singular* or *plural*.
Pronouns have PERSON. That is, pronouns can be the <u>first</u> person, or the <u>second</u> person, or the <u>third</u> person.

12

    Now, let's review the boring stuff, just to make sure:

    The first person singular is "I". The first person plural is "we".
    The second person singular is "you". In English the second person plural is also "you".
    The third person singular is "he, she" or "it". The third person plural is "they".

    Try to remember that. Then you won't ever have to read it again.

13

    Verbs are exactly the same. They have number (singular or plural) and person (first, second, or third).

    Introibo is in the first person singular. The *-bo-* at the end tells you that.

    But something is missing. There is something that we haven't talked about yet.

    Verbs also have **TIME.**

    Introibo is in <u>future time</u>. It means *I <u>shall</u> go in*.

14

    We shall talk about TIME in the next lesson.
    You have done very well. You deserve a rest and some hot chocolate.

Review Exercises

Here are 12 English pronouns arranged in a grid.

A	Singular	Plural
1st person	**I**	**we**
2nd person	**thou**	**you**
3rd person	**he**	**they**

B	Singular	Plural
1st person	**me**	**us**
2nd person	**thee**	**you**
3rd person	**him**	**them**

Questions:

1. Which pronoun occurs twice in the grid?
2. How many times would it occur, if we replaced *thou* and *thee* with modern forms?

Choose a pronoun from group A to complete these sentences:

3. Blessed art...........among women.
4. *Introibo* means "........ will go in".

Choose a pronoun from group B to complete these sentences:

5. The mail-man is here. I see .....
6. The boy-scouts are here. I see .....

Lesson 8: <u>Tense</u>

1

    Verbs have different TIMES.

    The English word for that idea is TENSE. We can say, "*Introibo* is in future time". Or we can say, "*Introibo* is in the future tense". Same thing.

2

    There are several different TENSES in English and in Latin. We are going to talk about three of them.

    Those three are:
    1. The <u>present</u> tense,
    2. the <u>past</u> tense, and
    3. the <u>future</u> tense.

3

    Here is an example of the <u>present</u> tense:

I am skating slowly, because my big toe hurts.

I am skating slowly [right now],
    because my big toe hurts [right now]. Ouch!

    How many verbs are there in that sentence? (Don't just read the question. Answer it!)

4

Here is a hard problem. You can skip it and go on to section 8 of this lesson, if you don't like puzzles.

We have said that a word is a verb, if you can put *we* in front of it and make sense. For example, *eat* is a verb, because you can say *we eat* and make sense. And *hockey* is not a verb, because you can not say *we hockey* and make sense.

Now by that test there are NO verbs in the sentence,
I am skating slowly, because my big toe hurts.

You can not say, "We am".
You can not say, "We skating".
You can not say, "We am skating".
And you can not say, "We hurts".

Something is wrong here. A happy sentence ought to have a verb, particularly if we are saying that the verb—which seems not to be there—is in the present tense.

5

Suppose we try to solve this problem by looking the words up in a dictionary. We will look up three words: *am*, *skating*, and *hurts*.

Oops! More grief! The words are not in the dictionary.

Depending on which dictionary you use, you might find *am*; but you will not find *skating* or *hurts*. And even if you do find *am*, you will then be told that you have gone to the wrong place, because you should have looked under *be*.

Am is under *be*. And *skating* and *hurts* are not there at all.

6

By now you probably know the answer, and you may be feeling impatient: If you want to look words up in an English dictionary, then you have to use the dictionary form of the word.

The dictionary form of *skating* is *skate*. And *skate* is indeed in the dictionary. The dictionary form of *hurts* is *hurt*. And *hurt* is also in the dictionary.

And *skate* and *hurt* are both verbs, because you can say *we skate* or *we hurt* and make sense.

7

What about *am*?

Am is a form of the verb *be*. (The verb *be* is usually called the verb *to be*. Same thing.)

The verb *to be* is a juvenile delinquent with a long record of misbehaviour.

And that is why we say, that the verb *to be* is an irregular verb.

Irregular verbs do not follow the rules.

8

We were talking about tense. We mentioned three tenses: the present, the past, and the future. We looked at a sentence with verbs in the present tense:

I am skating slowly, because my big toe hurts.

Now here are two examples of the future tense:

Tomorrow I shall be twelve years old.
Next week they will win the game.

We saw that *-bo-* was a marker of the future tense in Latin. The markers of the future tense in English are *shall* and *will*.

9

Shall and *will* are called "helper verbs", because they help you to form the future tense in English. They are also called "auxiliary verbs".

10

We were talking about **tense**. We mentioned three tenses: the present, the past, and the future.

We looked at a sentence with verbs in the present tense:
I am skating slowly, because my big toe hurts.

Then we looked at two examples of the future tense:
Tomorrow I shall be twelve years old.
Next week they will win the game.

Now we have one more tense to look at: the past tense.

11

The past tense is actually a family with a lot of members. Here are some examples

I played hockey. I have played. I did play. I was playing. I used to play. I had played.

Despite their differences, all of these are forms of the past tense.

12
How can I tell what tense a verb is in?

Easy! Just ask *when?*

"I am skating".
When?
Right now! Present tense.

"I shall win the game".
When?
Next Saturday! Future tense.

"I scored two goals".
When?
Last week! Past tense.

Review Exercises

1. Explain to somebody in your family—your little sister, if you have one—what we mean, when we say that

     VERBS have TENSE.

2. In the following sentences name the tense of the verbs:

a. I <u>read</u> this book last year.

b. I <u>want</u> to learn Latin, but I <u>am</u> too busy with hockey.

c. I <u>will finish</u> tomorrow.

Lesson 9: The Accusative Case

1

We have completed eight lessons. We have laid the foundation. From now on we are going to move forward more quickly.

But first, a short review:

In Latin, and in English, there are eight parts of speech. We have looked at five of them. The five are:

Noun
Pronoun
Adjective
Preposition
Verb

You should be able to explain all five of those parts of speech to somebody who is younger than you.

2

There are three parts of speech that we have not looked at, because they are too easy. Here they are:

Interjection. Interjections are words like *ouch* and *wow*. There are no interjections in the text of the Mass.

Conjunction. Conjunctions are little words like *and, but, if, when, while*, and so on.

Adverb. Adverbs like to go with verbs, for example: "I skate *fast*, I skate *slowly*, I skate *well*", and so forth. In English, adverbs often (but not always) end in –*ly*. Adverbs never change their form, not even in Latin.

3

    Priest: Introibo ad altare Dei.
    Server: Ad Deum qui laetificat juventutem meam.

What does *introibo* mean?

If (conjunction) **you** (pronoun) **have forgotten** (verb phrase in the past tense), then turn back a few pages to Lesson 7, and refresh your memory.

4

Ad altare means *to the altar*

There is no word for "the" in Latin.
Altare means *altar*.
Ad means *to*.

5

Ad is a preposition.
We have already seen another Latin preposition, *in*. We saw it in the phrase *in nomine*.
In and *ad* are both prepositions. But they are followed by different cases.

6

Help! What are cases? I don't remember what cases are. (The answer is in Lesson 3, section 5. Take a look if you need to.)

Cases are the different forms of a noun, pronoun, or adjective.

The nominative case is the dictionary form.
The genitive case is the "of-form".
The dative case is...., oops, we haven't done the dative case yet.
The accusative case is...., oops again. We haven't done that either.
The ablative case is used after the preposition *in*.

7

    The <u>accusative</u> case is used after the preposition *ad*.

    So *altare* is in the accusative case.

    By good luck the accusative case of *altare* and the nominative case are the same. So if you look *altare* up in a dictionary, you will find it.

8

Ad altare Dei means *to the altar of God.*

Dei means *of God.*

Dei is the "of-form". *Dei* is in the genitive case.
The nominative case—or the dictionary form—is *Deus*.

9

Ad Deum qui

Ad Deum means *to God.*
Ad means *to. Deum* means *God.*
Deum is in the accusative case, because it comes after the preposition *ad*.

    The nominative case of *Deum* is *Deus*.

Qui means *who.*

10

    Words like *qui* and *who* are called <u>relative pronouns</u>. You don't have to remember that.

Ad Deum qui means To God who.....

11

    Did you notice something odd?
Ad altare is different from *ad Deum*.
The ending *-re* is different from the ending *-um*.

    Altare and *Deum* both come after *ad*. And they are both in the accusative case. And they have different endings. Why is that?

12

    In Lesson 5 we talked about "case-families". Nouns in different case-families have have different endings.

    Case-families are called "declensions". There are five declensions in Latin.

    Deus is in the second declension. In the second declension the accusative ends in *-um*. So the accusative of *deus* is *deum*.

    Altare is in the third declension. And *altare* is a neuter noun. The accusative of any neuter noun is always the same as the nominative. Always. So the accusative of *altare* is *altare*.

    Deum and *altare* are both in the accusative case, but these two nouns belong to different declensions.

13

    Now we just said that *altare* was a neuter noun.
Neuter.
What does that mean?

14

If you speak French or Spanish or Italian, you already know that nouns have *gender*. A noun is either masculine or feminine.

For example, in French *le garçon* is masculine and *la maison* is feminine. *Le garçon* means "the boy". *La maison* means "the house".

In Latin—and in German and in Russian—there are three genders: masculine, feminine, and neuter. If you think Latin is tricky, think of this: In German there are 24 different ways to say "the". How many ways are there in Latin?

Deus is a masculine noun of the second declension. *Deum* is the accusative of *deus*.

Altare is a neuter noun of the third declension. *Altare* is the accusative of *altare*.

We have not yet seen a feminine noun.

15

What does *Introibo ad altare Dei* mean?

What does *Ad Deum qui* mean?

If you are not sure, look back and find the answers.

If you are sure that you know the answers, then you are ready for the next lesson.

Review Exercise

Translate the following into Latin:

1. to the altar

2. to God

3. to the altar of God

4. I shall go in

5. I shall go in to the altar of God.

Lesson 10: <u>Qui laetificat juventutem meam</u>

1

Qui means who.   (*Qui* and *who* are relative pronouns.)

laetificat is a verb.

Qui laetificat means "who gladdens", or "who gives joy to".

The dictionary form of *laetificat* is *laetifico*.

Laetifico means "gladden" or "make happy" or "give joy to".

Laetificat (with *-at* at the end) is the form that goes with *qui*.

2
   In the relative clause, *qui laetificat juventutem meam*, the verb *laetificat* is followed by an object in the accusative case.
   Now we have just used three new terms that you do not yet know. So let's get acquainted.

   "Clause"
   A "clause" is a sequence of words with a verb. Or, if you like, a clause is a small sentence. For example, here is a sentence with two clauses, "Aedan walked in, and Elise sat down".

   "Relative clause"
   A "relative clause" is a clause that begins with a relative pronoun. For example, "Any boy <u>who scores three goals</u> will win a prize".

   Now we need to find out what an "object" is.

3

    Let's start with three examples:

Aedan played hockey.
Elise eats veggies.
Katherine saw a grinch.

Those three sentences all have the same general form:

Noun - Verb - Noun

    The first noun—the noun before the verb—is the *subject*.

    Which word is the subject in each of those three examples?
(And remember: Don't just read the question. Answer it!)

    Did you get them right? If you did, then you are ready for the next challenge.

    The noun *after* the verb is the object. So now please identify (out loud!) the object in each sentence.

4

    The object of the verb is usually called the "direct object", because—as we shall see later—there is another little critter called an "indirect object". We'll talk about that later, on page 115.

5

    Now let's do some pretend grammar. Imagine that there is an English word **"to verb"**.
    For example, here are some sentences using this new word.

We all verb ice-cream.
Aedan verbed Elise right on the nose.
I'm going to verb a book about snakes.

    What is the subject in each sentence? What is the direct object? How do you know?
    (Guess what! You're supposed to <u>answer</u> those questions.)

6

The direct object of a sentence is the person or thing that **gets verbed**.

The subject of a sentence is the person or thing that **does** the **verbing**.

In English the subject of a sentence usually comes first. It comes *before* the verb.

In English the direct object of a sentence usually comes third. It comes *after* the verb.

7

In Latin the direct object is always in the accusative case. Word-order doesn't matter at all.

Juventutem meam is the direct object of *laetificat*. That's why *juventutem meam* is in the accusative case.

Laetificat juventutem meam means "gladdens my youth", or "makes my youth happy".

8

In Latin the subject of the verb is usually in the nominative case. Word-order still doesn't matter.

So now we know what the nominative case is used for. It isn't just used for looking words up in the dictionary.

<u>The nominative case is used to identify the subject of the verb.</u>

PS: Do you remember that in Lesson 3 in section 6, we said that we didn't know what the nominative case was used for? Well, now we do know. The nominative case marks the subject.

9

Ad Deum qui laetificat

Qui is a relative pronoun. It is in the nominative case. It is the subject of the verb *laetificat*. It means "who".

Laetificat is a verb in the third person singular in the present tense. It means "gladdens".

Ad Deum qui laetificat means "to God who gladdens".

10

Juventutem meam means "youth my". Of course, in English we say that the other way around. We say, "my youth". Same thing.

11

Meam is a possessive adjective.

A possessive adjective is an adjective whose job is to tell you who owns the noun. Whose youth are we talking about here? We are talking about MY youth.

Juventutem means "youth".
Meam means "my".
Juventutem meam means "my youth".

12

What does *Qui laetificat juventutem meam* mean?
(Answer, please!)

13

What does *Ad Deum qui laetificat juventutem meam* mean?
(Answer, please!)

Review Exercises

1. Read and then translate out loud: *In nomine Patris et Filii et Spiritus sancti, Amen. Introibo ad altare Dei, Ad Deum qui laetificat juventutem meam.*

2. Translate into Latin:

> I gladden.

(Hint: What is the dictionary form of *laetificat*?)

Lesson 11: <u>Judica me, Deus</u>

1

Me in Latin means "me" in English. *Me* means "me". Who said Latin was hard?

2

Judica is a verb. It means, "Judge!". It is in the command-form. The command-form is used for giving an order or for making a request. It is called the <u>imperative.</u> *Judica* is in the imperative.

The dictionary form of *judic<u>a</u>* is *judic<u>o</u>*.

Did you put the accent on the ending just then? Try not to do that. The accent of *judica* belongs on the first syllable. That's why in the Missal it is written like this: Júdica. The little accent mark tells you which syllable is the loudest.

Judica me means "judge me".

3

What is missing here?
A <u>subject</u> is missing. There is no subject.
In English and in Latin, when we give an order or make a request, the verb has no subject.

For example, we can say,
Aedan is eating his broccoli.
"Aedan" is the subject.

But if we say,
Hey Aedan, eat your broccoli!
there is no spoken subject.

Same in Latin and English.

4

Deus looks as if it is in the nominative case. But remember that the nominative case is used for marking the subject of a sentence. And this time there is no subject, because the verb is imperative. So *Deus* can't be in the nominative case.

Deus is in the <u>vocative</u> case. In Latin the vocative case is easy, because it almost always has the same form as the nominative case.

5

We use the vocative case in Latin in order to name the person that we are talking TO.

In English we sometimes say "Hey" first. For example,

Hey Aedan, eat your broccoli !

But the word "hey" is not exactly polite. So when we are praying, we can use the old-fashioned word "O". (You can also spell that "Oh".) For example,

Oh Lord,
O my Jesus,
O God.

6

Judica me, Deus

means

Judge me, O God

If you prefer, you can skip the word "O", and just say: *Judge me, God*. But some people think it sounds nice to say, "O". It's your choice.

7

Do you remember what *et* means? If you've forgotten, turn back a few pages and find the answer.

8

Et discerne causam meam

Discerne is a verb. It means "distinguish".

Discerne is in the command-form. The command-form is used for giving an order or making a request. The command-form is called the <u>imperative</u>. *Discerne* is in the imperative.

The dictionary-form of *discerne* is *discerno*.

9

Did you notice a small difference between *discerne* and *judica*?

They are both in the command-form. But *discerne* ends in –*e*, and *judica* ends in –*a*.

Why is that?

10

We noticed something similar with nouns.

For example, *patris*, and *filii*, and *spiritūs* have different endings. Nonetheless, they are all in the <u>of-form</u>. That is to say, they are all in the genitive case.

We talked about "case-families". Case-families are called "declensions". There are five different declensions in Latin. The nouns *pater*, and *filius*, and *spiritus* belong to different declensions. And so they make their of-form differently.

11

Families of **verbs** are called "conjugations". There are four conjugations.

Judico is in the <u>first</u> conjugation. In the first conjugation the command-form (or the imperative) is *judica,* with an –*a*.

Discerno is in the <u>third</u> conjugation. In the third conjugation the imperative is *discerne* with an –*e*.

12

    Do I have to remember all this STUFF ?

    Nope. The grammar is only there in order to help you understand the Latin words.

    You don't have to remember the grammar. But you should try to understand it. If you don't understand the grammar, ask for help. There are no dumb questions. Asking questions is smart.

13

    What do I have to remember?

    You have to remember what the Latin words mean. Nothing else.

14

Et discerne causam meam

means

"And distinguish my cause".

15

    Causam meam means "cause my". But in English, of course, we say "my cause".

    What does *juventutem meam* mean? If you have forgotten, turn back a few pages and look it up.

    Causam and *juventutem* are both in the accusative singular. They have different endings, because they belong to different declensions.

16

    Causam meam is a noun-phrase in the accusative singular. *Causam* is the direct object of *discerne*.

17

Meam is a possessive adjective. *Meam* modifies *causam*. We can also say, "*Meam* agrees with *causam*", or "*Meam* goes with *causam*". Same thing.

Causam meam means "my cause". *Et discerne causam meam* means "and distinguish my cause".

18

Read the following Latin words out loud. Then translate them into English. If you have difficulty, ask for help.

In nomine Patris et Filii et Spiritus sancti, Amen.

Introibo ad altare Dei,
Ad Deum qui laetificat juventutem meam.

Judica me, Deus, et discerne causam meam.....

Review Exercises

Translate the following into Latin. Any correct form will be acceptable.

1. name

2. holy

3. I will go in

4. altar

5. God

6. youth

7. judge

8. distinguish

9. cause

10. my

Lesson 12: <u>de gente non sanctā</u>

1

Discerne causam meam

"Distinguish my cause"

De gente non sancta

"from the nation that is not holy".

2

De means "from".

Gente means "nation" or "people"

De is a preposition, and it takes the ablative case. *Gente* is a noun in the ablative case. *Gente* also happens to be feminine.

De gente means "from the nation", or "from a people".

As you can see, there is more than one right way to translate these words. You never have to memorise a particular translation. Since you understand the Latin text, you are allowed to use your own words, when you translate.

3

Can you guess what *non* means?
Careful! It does not mean, "No".

4

Sancta is an adjective.
Sancta is feminine and ablative. It goes with *gente*, because *gente* is a feminine noun in the ablative case. We need not bother with the dictionary form of *gente*.
Have you noticed that Latin adjectives often come AFTER the noun they modify? In English, an adjective usually comes before its noun.
Gente non sancta means "a people not holy".

5

De gente non sancta means "from a people not holy", or "from the nation that is not holy".

Look at the underlined words, "that is". Those words are not actually in the Latin text. The English translator put them in, because he thought it sounded better.

When you are translating, you can put words like that in, or you can leave them out. It's up to you.

6

We have now seen the Latin adjective meaning "holy" three times.

Do you remember the other two times? Give yourself a gold star if you can remember both of them.

7

Do you remember these next words? They actually belong to the blessing at the end of Mass. We saw them in Lesson 2.

Benedicat vos omnipotens Deus:
Pater et Filius et Spiritus Sanctus.

What does the second line—*Pater et Filius et Spiritus Sanctus*—mean?

(Always read the Latin words out loud, and give the required translation into English out loud, please!)

8

Can you translate these three phrases into English?

Spiritus Sanctus
Spiritūs Sancti
de gente non sanctā

What are three different ways to say "holy" in Latin? (Yes, of course, say them out loud!)

9

What do you think *omnipotens Deus* means? You probably know the word *Deus*. Think of an English word that is similar to *omnipotens*. Now guess what *omnipotens Deus* means.
What is your guess?

10

We have now seen the word for *God* three times. Can you supply the missing form of *Deus* in the other two?

(1) *Introibo ad altare..........*
      and
(2) *Ad......... qui laetificat*

If you are sure of the answer, write it down. If you are not sure, look it up.

11

Ab homine iniquo et doloso erue me.

Ab is a preposition. *Ab* means "from". *Ab* takes the ablative case. (As we have seen, *de* also means "from".)
Now we need to find a noun in the ablative case.

12

Homine is a noun in the ablative case. *Homine* is masculine and singular. *Homine* means "man".

The nominative case of *homine* is *homo*. The nominative case occurs in the Creed, during the part where we genuflect: *et homo factus est*.

Ab homine means "from a man" or "from the man".

13

Iniquo and *doloso* are adjectives. They are singular. They are masculine. And they are in the ablative case.

What noun in the text do they modify, or "go with"? How do you know?

Iniquo means "wicked", or "unjust".
Doloso means "deceitful" or "tricky".

Ab homine iniquo et doloso means "from a man wicked and deceitful", or (if you prefer), "from the unjust and deceitful man".

14

The dictionary form of any adjective is the nominative, masculine, singular. (Yes, of course, adjectives also have feminine, and neuter, and plural forms.)

The nominative, masculine singular of *iniquo* is iniquus. The nominative, masculine singular of *doloso* is dolosus.

Iniquus and *dolosus* are adjectives of the second declension. That means that they belong to the same case-family as *Deus*. The dictionary-form of words in the second declension almost always ends in -*us*.

Iniquus means "wicked". If you already know the English word "iniquity", you should find it easy to remember what *iniquus* means.

There is no easy way to remember the meaning of *dolosus*. It means "tricky", and it can be tricky to remember.

15

Ab homine iniquo et doloso is a prepositional phrase. Please translate it into English.

16

Erue me.

Erue is a verb. *Erue* is in the command-form, or the imperative. The dictionary-form *erue* is *eruo*.

Erue means "deliver" or "rescue".

Erue me means "deliver me", or "rescue me".

17

Now you can translate the whole clause into English: *Ab homine iniquo et doloso erue me.*

18

Read the following Latin words out loud. Slowly. Then translate them into English. If you need to look back to an earlier page to find an answer, you are perfectly free to do so.

In nomine Patris et Filii et Spiritus sancti, Amen.

Introibo ad altare Dei,
Ad Deum qui laetificat juventutem meam.

Judica me, Deus, et discerne causam meam de gente non sanctā. Ab homine iniquo et doloso erue me.

If it would help you to write down the answers, go ahead. This is your book, and you are encouraged to write notes in it.

Review Exercises

Translate into Latin:

1. Judge me, O God.

2. Distinguish my cause.

3. Rescue me.

4. Rescue me from the wicked man. (Use *ab*)

5. Deliver me from the nation [that is] not holy. (Use *de*)

PS: You do not need to translate the words in square brackets.

Lesson 13: <u>Quia tu es Deus</u>

1

Quia tu es, Deus, fortitudo mea.

"Because, O God, you are my strength", or "For you, O God, are my strength".

2

Quia means "because" or "for"

Tu es means "you are".
Tu means "you". *Es* means "are".

Deus means "God" or "O God".

3

Fortitudo is a noun. It means "strength".
You can remember the meaning of *fortitudo* by thinking of the English word "fortitude".

Fortitudo mea means "my strength".

Fortitudo is in the nominative case. However, it is <u>not</u> the subject of the sentence.
The nominative case has another use. We use the nominative case <u>after</u> the verb *to be*.

Which of the following do you prefer,

It is I or *It is me* ?

In Latin there is no choice here. You have to use the nominative.

4

What does *quia tu es Deus, fortitudo mea* mean?

Always give the answer out loud, please.

5

Translate these three Latin noun phrases:

juventutem meam
causam meam
fortitudo mea.

Look back a few pages if you do not remember the answer.

6

Quare me repulisti.

Repulisti is a verb. Let's compare it to the verb *introibo*.

Introibo means "I will go in". But the Latin word for "I", namely *ego*, is not there.
Repulisti means "you rejected". And the Latin word for "you", namely *tu*, is also not there.

7

Introibo is a verb in the 1st person singular. And it is in the future tense.
Repulisti is a verb in the 2nd person singular. And it is in the past tense.

-bo means "I, and future tense". For example, *lavabo* means "I will wash". Where have you seen the word *lavabo*?
-isti means "you, and past tense". For example, *venisti* means "you came".

8

    Latin verbs include a silent personal pronoun such as *I, you,* or *he* and so forth. If there is no <u>noun</u> in the nominative case, then the silent <u>pronoun</u> will be the subject.

    Lavabo = ego lavabo = I will wash.

    and

    Repulisti = tu repulisti = you rejected.

9

    Me repulisti means "you rejected me".

    Quare means "why?".

10

    What does *quare me repulisti* mean?

11

    Did your answer sound like normal modern English? If so, fine. If not, please correct it.

12

    Here are two incomplete translations of *Quare repulisti me*. Please complete them by putting in the missing words:

    "Why have you..... ?
    "Why did you.... ?

13

    Here is a statement: "It is raining".
    And here is a question: "Is it raining?"

    Here is another statement: "You did go."
    And here is another question: "Did you go?"

    Now please describe one way to turn a statement into a question in English.

    That method does not exist in Latin. In Latin the word-order of a statement and the word-order of a question are exactly the same.

14

    Translate these words into English:

    Quia tu es Deus, fortitudo mea. Quare me repulisti?

15

Et quare tristis incedo

    What does *et quare* mean?

    Tristis means "sorrowing", or "sorrowful". *Tristis* is an adjective.

    Incedo is a verb. It means "I go".

    The dictionary-form of any Latin verb is the "I-form", or the first person singular of the present tense. And this is the first time that we have seen a verb in its dictionary-form. The dictionary-form of a Latin verb will almost always end in -o.

    Do you remember the dictionary-form of *laetificat*? Or *judica*? Or *discerne*? Or *erue*? If you don't remember the forms, figure them out right now. It's easy.

16
    Both in English and in Latin a verb can be followed by an adverb. For example:

Aedan ran quickly.

Which word in that sentence is an adverb?

17
    But both in English and in Latin a few verbs can be followed by an adjective instead of by an adverb. For example:

Aedan plays rough.
Aedan left hungry.

Rough and *hungry* are adjectives. Name the two adverbs related to *rough* and *hungry*.

18
    Tristis incedo means "I go sorrowful". *Tristis* is an adjective.

    Suppose we say that *tristis* means "sad", and *incedo* means "I go around". Then what will *tristis incedo* mean? What will *Quare tristis incedo* mean?

    Did your answer sound like normal modern English? If not, please correct it.

19
    Translate these words into English:

Quia tu es Deus, fortitudo mea.
Quare me repulisti,
et quare tristis incedo....?

20

Dum affligit me inimicus

Dum means "while".
What does *me* mean?

Inimicus means "enemy" or "the enemy". It is a noun in the nominative case. It is the subject of the verb *affligit*.

21
    So now we have a clause with four words, and we know what three of the four words mean:

    Dum affligit me inimicus   means
  "while the enemy affligit me".

22
    Now try to guess what *affligit* means. Any good guess will be acceptable.
    Write down your guess.

23
    Now look in your missal, and figure out what *affligit* means. Write down the answer.

    How close was your guess?

    What does *affligit* mean in modern English?

    What is the dictionary-form of *affligit*? What does it mean?

24

    Read these words out, and then translate them into English. Use your own words when you translate.

    Quare tristis incedo, dum affligit me inimicus?

25

    Now do the whole verse:

    Quia tu es Deus, fortitudo mea.
    Quare me repulisti, et quare tristis incedo,
    dum affligit me inimicus?

26

    Good for you!

Review Exercises

Translate into Latin:

1. my youth (accusative case)

2. my cause (accusative case)

3. my strength (nominative case)

4. You are sad.

5. I shall go in sad.

6. You rejected me.

7. The enemy afflicts me.

8. while

9. because

10. why?

Lesson 14: <u>Emitte lucem tuam</u>

1

Emitte means "send forth", or "send out".

Emitte is a verb. It is in the imperative, or the command-form.

What is the dictionary-form of *emitte*? What does the dictionary-form mean? Is there a similar and useful English word?

2

Lucem tuam means "your light" or "thy light".

Lucem tuam is a noun-phrase in the accusative case.

3

Et veritatem tuam

The noun *veritatem* is another noun in the accusative case. You already know what *tuam* means. *Veritatem* means "truth".

What does the noun-phrase *veritatem tuam* mean?

4

The whole noun-phrase *lucem tuam et veritatem tuam* is the direct object of the verb *emitte*.

Say and translate:
lucem tuam et veritatem tuam

Say and translate:
Emitte lucem tuam et veritatem tuam.

(Out loud, please! You can also write down the answers, if you wish.)

5
     Say these noun-phrases out loud. Then translate them into English:

juventutem meam
causam meam
fortitudo mea
lucem tuam
veritatem tuam

     Which one of them is NOT in the accusative case?
     Which two of the possessive adjectives are NOT in the first person singular? Which person are they in?

6
Ipsa me deduxerunt et adduxerunt

     Ipsa is a pronoun. *Ipsa* is plural, and it is in the nominative case.
     Ipsa means "they".

     The English third-person plural pronoun "they" is in the nominative (or "subjective") case. What is the accusative (or "objective") case of this <u>English</u> pronoun?

     Use the third-person plural pronoun in English to complete these sentences:

.........*are here.*

I see......

7
     From now on you will get no more help with the Latin words *me* and *et*. You are on your own.

8

deduxērunt et adduxērunt

These are both verbs. They are both in the third-person plural. (Another way to explain that, is to say that they are both in the "they-form".) And they are both in the past tense.

The dictionary-form of *deduxērunt* is *dedūco*. What is the dictionary-form of *adduxērunt*?

Deduco means "lead" or "conduct".

Adduco means "bring". (What is the past tense of *bring*?)

9

Ipsa me deduxerunt et adduxerunt

Here is a partial translation:

"They have *verbed* me and *verbed* me".

As you can see, we are allowed to say "me" twice in English, even though we only said it once in Latin.

Now please take out the temporary word *verbed*, and replace it with the proper English words in the right form.

If you have any trouble doing that, then look the answer up in your missal. Did you get the right answer?

10

Say these words in Latin:

ipsa me deduxerunt et adduxerunt

Now translate them into English.

11

in montem sanctum tuum et in tabernacula tua

There are two prepositional phrases here:

    in montem sanctum tuum

and

    in tabernacula tua.

They are both followed by the accusative case. Do you remember the first prepositional phrase that we looked at?

in nomine

In that phrase, the preposition *in* was followed by the ablative case. Whenever the Latin preposition *in* simply means "in" in English, it will be followed by the ablative case.

However, in these two new phrases the meaning of *in* is different. Now *in* means "to" (or *onto*, or *unto*, or *into*). When the Latin preposition *in* means "to" in English, then it is followed by the accusative case.

In + accusative expresses <u>motion</u> toward some place.

12

in montem sanctum tuum

Montem is in the accusative case, and it means "mountain".

We can translate the preposition *in* here either as "unto", or as "onto". They are both correct.

You already know what *sanctum* and *tuum* mean. They go with *montem*, and all three of those words are in the masculine accusative singular.

So what does *in montem sanctum tuum* mean in English? If you need any help, just ask. If you can do it by yourself, all the better.

13
> *in tabernacula tua*

In this phrase the noun *tabernacula* means "tabernacles", and the preposition *in* means "to" or "into".

So what does *in tabernacula tua* mean?

14
> The word "tabernacle" here does not refer to a strong-box on the altar, where the Blessed Sacrament is kept. It means the place on earth where God dwells. The original meaning of the word was "tent".

15
> Now let's put the whole verse together. Look back whenever you want to. This is not a memory test. Say the words carefully in Latin. Then translate them into English. Do one line at a time, or do the whole thing at once, as you prefer. If you have any difficulty, it might be a good idea to write down part of your answer. Then you will be able to refer to your notes later, if need arises.

Emitte lucem tuam et veritatem tuam.

Ipsa me deduxerunt et adduxerunt

in montem sanctum tuum

et in tabernacula tua.

Review Exercises

Translate into Latin:

1. Send forth

2. your light (accusative case)

3. and your truth (accusative case)

4. Send forth your light and your truth.

5. They have led me.

6. to your holy mountain

7. and to your tabernacles

8. They have led me and brought [me].

Lesson 15: Confitebor

1 *Confitēbor* is a verb in the "I-will" form. In other words it is

<u>first person singular</u>, and <u>future tense</u>.

In that respect it is just like *introibo*.

Introibo means "I will go in". And *confitēbor* means "I will praise".

But it has an "r" at the end! If it were exactly like *introibo*, then it would be <u>confitebo</u> with no "r" at the end. What gives?

Confitebor likes to have an "r". The present tense of *confitebor* is *confiteo<u>r</u>*. And there is that "r" again! Verbs that behave like this are called "deponent". Deponent verbs like to have an "r".

The dictionary form of *confitebor* is *confiteor*.

2 And now we have a problem.

Confitebor means "I will praise". But in the Mass the present tense of this verb, *confiteor,* means "I confess".
Does this verb change its meaning, when it changes tense? No one should be allowed to behave like that!

The answer is very simple. This verb has two meanings. And you get to choose whichever meaning fits best in a particular sentence.

Confiteor means either "I praise", or "I confess".

Confitebor means either "I will praise", or "I will confess".

They are both correct, and your choice will depend on the context.

3

Confitebor tibi

Confitebor means "I will praise".

What is *tibi*?

Tibi means "you".

Confitebor tibi means "I will praise you".

4

Let's look more closely at *tibi*.

First of all, do you remember these words:

Quia tu es Deus, fortitudo mea?

"because, O God, you are my strength"

What does *tu* mean?

If you don't remember the answer, look back and find it. Then write it down here:

tu means ....

5

Tu is the second-person singular pronoun, and it is in the nominative case.

Tibi is in the dative case. *Tibi* is the dative of *tu*.

The dative case of any noun—or pronoun or adjective—can be called the
> "to-form".

If I give something <u>to Aedan,</u> then Aedan will be in the dative case.

6

    The verb *confiteor* likes to be followed by the dative case. So *tibi* here is the object of *confitebor*.

    And we can translate *confitebor tibi* as:

"I will give praise <u>to you</u>".

    You could also say, "I will praise you", because that means pretty much the same thing.

7

    Please observe the accented syllable.
(If you don't remember what that means, look on page 17.)

confitebor is accented like this: confitEbor

confiteor is accented like this: confIteor

    In your Missal they are written with an accent mark:

confitébor   and   confíteor

    You will not forget how to pronounce *confiteor*, because the word is familiar. If you forget how to pronounce *confitebor*, just look for the accent mark in your Missal.

    If you find it helpful to write accent marks in this book, go right ahead.

    As it happens, the [e] in *confitebor* is a long vowel. So we can also write the word like this:

confitēbor

8

Let's review the cases:

The <u>nominative</u> case is used to mark the subject of a sentence, and it is also used after the verb *to be*. For example: <u>*tu*</u> *es* <u>*Deus*</u>. Why are both of those words underlined?

The <u>genitive</u> case is the "of-case". It is used to show possession. For example: *in nomine* <u>*Patris*</u>. What does that mean?

The <u>dative</u> case is the "to-case". And it is also used after the verb *confiteor*. For example: *confitebor* <u>*tibi*</u>.

The <u>accusative</u> case marks the direct object of a verb. And the accusative is always used after the preposition *ad*. And it is also used after the preposition *in*, when *in* means "to". For example: *in montem sanctum tuum*. What does that mean?

The <u>ablative</u> case is used after the preposition *in*, when *in* means "in" or "on". For example: *in* <u>*nomine*</u>

The <u>vocative</u> case is used to name the person to whom we are speaking. The vocative almost always has the same form as the nominative.

7

What does *confitebor tibi* mean?

(Out loud, as usual, please. Or write the answers down, as you prefer.)

8

in citharā

in means "on"

cithara is a noun in the ablative case. *cithara* means "harp".

What does *in cithara* mean?

9
    Translate these words and phrases into English:

    i. Quare tristis incedo

    ii. es

    iii. quare tristis es

10

    Anima mea means "O my soul". It is in the vocative case. The psalmist is speaking to his soul.

11
    Conturbas means "you upset" or "you disquiet".

    Conturbas is a verb in the 2nd person singular of the present tense.

    What is the dictionary form of *conturbas*?

Here are two different translations of *quare conturbas me.*

i. *why dost thou disquiet me?*

ii. *why are you bugging me?*

Are they both right? Which one do you prefer?

12
>Say these words out loud, and then translate them into English.

>*Confitebor tibi in cithara, Deus Deus meus.*

>*Quare tristis es, anima mea? et quare conturbas me?*

13
>How many vocatives are there in those two sentences? Please underline them. To whom is the psalmist speaking in the first sentence? To whom is he speaking in the second sentence?

14 Read the following Latin words out loud. Slowly. Then translate them into English. If you have difficulty, ask for help. If you miss anything, make a note for yourself on this page near the word.

In nomine Patris et Filii et Spiritus sancti, Amen.

Introibo ad altare Dei,
Ad Deum qui laetificat juventutem meam.

Judica me, Deus, et discerne causam meam de gente non sanctā. Ab homine iniquo et doloso erue me.

Quia tu es Deus, fortitudo mea. Quare me repulisti? Et quare tristis incedo, dum affligit me inimicus?

Review Exercises

Translate into Latin:

1. I will go in

2. I will praise you

3. on a harp

4. O God, my God

5. Why art thou sad, O my soul?

6. And why dost thou disquiet me?

7. because, O God, you are my strength

8. Why have you rejected me?

9. The enemy afflicts me.

10. to God who gladdens my youth

Lesson 16: Spera in Deo

1

Spera in Deo, quoniam adhuc confitebor illi: salutare vultūs mei et Deus meus.

Spera is a verb. *Spera* is in the command-form, or the imperative. *Spera* means "hope!".

What is the dictionary-form of *spera*? What does the dictionary-form mean?

Translate *Spera in Deo* into English.

2

Quoniam is a conjunction. *Quoniam* means "because" or "for". (If you have forgotten about conjunctions, they are on page 47.)

Adhuc is an adverb. *Adhuc* means "still".
(If you have forgotten about adverbs, they are also on page 47.)

3

Confitebor illi

Illi is a pronoun in the dative singular. *Illi* means "him" or "to him".

Translate:
Confitebor tibi

Translate:
Quoniam adhuc confitebor illi

4

Salutare vultūs mei

Salutare is a noun. *Salutare* means "salvation", or "the salvation".

5

Vultūs mei

Vultūs mei is a noun-phrase in the genitive case. Both words are in the genitive case. They have different endings because *vultūs* is a noun in the fourth declension (or case-family), while *mei* is in the second declension.

Mei has the same meaning as *meus*. *Mei* is the genitive of *meus*. Both words mean the same thing. They both mean "my".

Vultus (with a short "u") means "face". The genitive, or "of-form" is *vultūs*.

What does *vultūs mei* mean?

Write down another noun, which has the same endings as *vultus*. Hint: think of the sign of the cross.

6

Read the words out loud. Then translate them.

Spera in Deo, quoniam adhuc confitebor illi:

salutare vultūs mei et Deus meus.

Who is the psalmist talking to? That is, to whom is he saying, "Hope!"?

If you have any trouble, look back; and then write down a note to help yourself.

7

    Read out loud. Translate out loud. If you have any trouble, look the answer up, and then write down a note to help yourself.

Emitte lucem tuam et veritatem tuam. Ipsa me deduxerunt et adduxerunt in montem sanctum tuum et in tabernacula tua.

Et introibo ad altare Dei, ad Deum qui laetificat juventutem meam.

Confitebor tibi in cithara, Deus Deus meus. Quare tristis es, anima mea, et quare conturbas me?

Spera in Deo, quoniam adhuc confitebor illi: salutare vultūs mei et Deus meus.

8

    What are the eight parts of speech?

    PS: Next time you get this question, you have to know the complete answer.

Review Exercises

Translate into Latin:

1. Hope!

2. Hope in God!

3. I will praise you.

4. I will praise him.

5. the salvation of my face

6. of the Holy Spirit

7. of my spirit

8. Send forth your light and your truth.

9. to the altar

10. to God

Lesson 17: <u>Gloria Patri</u>

1

Gloria Patri et Filio et Spirítui Sancto

These words are a <u>sentence</u> without a verb. You will not need a verb in English either.

The subject of the sentence is *Gloria*. *Gloria* is a noun in the nominative case.

The remainder of the sentence is *Patri et Filio et Spirítui Sancto*.

<u>*Patri et Filio et Spirítui Sancto*</u> is a noun-phrase in the dative case. All the words—except *et*—are in the dative case. Remember: the dative case is the "to-case".

Here is an <u>in</u>complete translation:
"Glory to [noun-phrase in the dative case]".

If you want to supply a verb, you can say:
"Glory be to [noun-phrase in the dative case].

Now please translate the whole sentence.

2

    Write down the Latin for *Father and Son and Holy Ghost* in

The nominative case:

In the genitive case:

And in the dative case:

If you have to look an answer up, make a note of the page where you found it.

3
$$\begin{cases} eram = \text{I was} \\ eras = \text{you were} \\ erat = \text{it (or } he \text{ or } she\text{) was} \end{cases}$$

    What part of *erat* means "was"? What part of *erat* means "it"?

4

    Sicut erat in principio

    Sicut is a conjunction. *Sicut* means "as".

    What does *sicut erat* mean?

5

    Principio is the ablative of *principium*. *Principium* means "beginning". Why do we need the ablative case here?

    Translate *Sicut erat in principio*.

6

Et nunc et semper

Nunc means "now".
Semper means "forever", or "always".

What does *et nunc et semper* mean?

You may find that you want to translate the two "ets" (et....et) as "both....and": *both now and forever*.

7

Et in saecula saeculorum.

If we translate this phrase word-for-word, we get

"and unto the ages of ages".

Saecula is accusative plural, and *saeculorum* is genitive plural. So:
in saecula = unto the ages
saeculorum = *of ages*.

But we usually translate these words as

"world without end".

8

Some people translate *et nunc et semper* as "is now and ever shall be".

Which do you like better, a <u>literal translation</u> or a <u>free translation</u> ?

9

Adjutorium nostrum ✠ *in nomine Domini.*

✠ means: Make a sign of the cross here.

Adjutorium is a noun in the nominative case. *Adjutorium* means "help".

Based on your other knowledge, please guess what *adjutorium nostrum* means. Do you need a hint? *Pater noster* means "Our Father".

You already know *in nomine*. *Domini* is a new word for you. It is the genitive of *Dominus*. And you can guess what *Dominus* means. Need a hint? *Dominus vobiscum*.

Try to guess what *Adjutorium nostrum in nomine Domini* means.

Did you add the word *is* in English? As you may have noticed, Latin often omits the verb *to be*.

10

Qui fecit caelum et terram.

Qui means "who". *Qui* is a relative pronoun in the nominative case.

fecit = "made". *Fecit* is a verb in the past tense.

caelum et terram = "heaven and earth". Both nouns are in the accusative case.

Qui is the subject of *fecit*. The phrase *caelum et terram* is the direct object of *fecit*.

Translate: *Qui fecit caelum et terram.*

Review Exercises

Translate into Latin:

1. Glory [be] to the Father....

2. .... and to the Son and to the Holy Spirit

3. as it was in the beginning

4. both now and forever

5. our help

6. [is] in the name of the Lord

7. Our help [is] in the name of the Lord.

8. who made

9. who made heaven and earth

10. The Lord made the earth.

Lesson 18: <u>The Confiteor</u>

1   There are two main verbs in the *Confiteor*.
They are both "r-verbs", and so they end in "–or ".
The two verbs are *confiteor* (in the first part), and *precor* (in the second part).

2   *Confiteor* means "I confess".
Confiteor is followed by the dative case. The dative case is the "to-case".

The verb *confiteor* is here followed by several noun-phrases in the dative case. They belong to different "case-families", or declensions. Thus even though they all have <u>dative</u> endings, they do not all have the <u>same</u> endings.

Here they are:

i. *Deo omnipotenti*
   "to God almighty"

ii. *beatae Mariae semper Virgini*
   "to blessed Mary ever Virgin"

iii. *beato Michaëli Archangelo*
   "to blessed Michael the Archangel"

iv. *beato Joanni Baptistae*
   "to blessed John the Baptist"

v. <u>sanctis</u> *Apostolis Petro et Paulo*
   "to the holy Apostles Peter and Paul"

vi. *omnibus* <u>Sanctis</u>
   "to all the saints"

vii. *et tibi*
   "and to you"

Sanctis is an adjective meaning "holy". And *sanctis* is also a noun meaning "saints".

3

The priest is speaking to everybody. The server is speaking to the priest. So the wording is slightly different.

The priest says *et vobis, fratres*. That means, "and to you, brethren". *Vobis* is plural, and *fratres* is vocative.

The server says *et tibi, pater*. That means "and to you, father". *Tibi* is singular, and *pater* is vocative.

Et vobis, fratres	"and to you, brethren"
Et tibi, pater	"and to you, father"

Where have we seen *tibi* before? If you forget, find the answer and note the page.

4

Quia peccavi nimis

Quia is a conjunction. *Quia* means "that", or "because".

Peccavi is a verb in the past tense. *Peccavi* means "I have sinned". The dictionary form of *peccavi* is *pecco*. What does it mean?

Nimis is an adverb. *Nimis* means "exceedingly" or "a lot".

Say and translate:

Quia peccavi nimis

5

Cogitatione, verbo, et opere

"in thought, word, and deed"

Those three Latin nouns are in the ablative case. To translate them into English, we have to use the preposition "in".

cogitatione	"in thought"
verbo	"in word"
et opere	"and in deed"

Here is another translation of the same phrase. Of course, in private prayer you can use your own translation.

"in my thoughts, and in my words, and in my actions".

6

meā culpā, meā culpā,
  meā maximā culpā

What does *mea* mean?
Culpa is a noun. *Culpa* means "fault".

Maxima means "very great". In the Missal it is translated as "most grievous".

The phrase, *meā culpā, meā culpā, meā maximā culpā* is entirely in the ablative case. However, we need a preposition to translate it into English. The English preposition *through* fits well.

Translate the phrase into English. Try a different English preposition if you like.

7

Say these words out loud. Then translate them into English in your own words.

Confiteor.... quia peccavi nimis cogitatione, verbo, et opere: mea culpa, mea culpa, mea maxima culpa.

8

Now we can make the return trip.

Ideo precor

Ideo means "therefore".

Precor is an "r-verb". *Precor* means "I beg", or "I beseech".

What does *Ideo precor* mean?

9

Precor takes the accusative case. So all the saints who were in the dative case in the first part, will now be in the accusative case.

In the second part of the *Confiteor* we do not repeat "God almighty", because we are now begging all the saints to pray to God for us. So we start with the Blessed Virgin.

Here is the list:

i. [omitted]

ii. *beatam Mariam semper Virginem*
     "blessed Mary ever Virgin"

iii. *beatum Michaëlem Archangelum*
      "blessed Michael the Archangel"

iv. *beatum Joannem Baptistam*
     "blessed John the Baptist"

v. <u>*sanctos*</u> *Apostolos Petrum et Paulum*
    "the holy Apostles Peter and Paul"

vi. *omnes* <u>*Sanctos*</u>
     "all the saints"

vii. *et te*
      "and you"

10

First I confess: *confiteor*

Then I beg: *precor*

What do I beg for, or ask for?

I beg all the saints, together with the priest, TO PRAY FOR ME TO THE LORD OUR GOD.

Orare	to pray
pro me	for me
ad Dominum	to the Lord
Deum nostrum	our God

11
    Say these out loud. Then translate them.

Ideo precor..... omnes sanctos et vos, fratres, orare pro me.

Ideo precor..... omnes sanctos et te, pater, orare pro me.

12
    Orare, of course, is a verb. The form "orare" is called an <u>infinitive.</u>

    An infinitive in English almost always <u>begins</u> with the word "to". For example: *to skate, to shoot, to score, to win.*

    An infinitive in Latin almost always <u>ends</u> with the letters "-re".

    So *orare* is an infinitive. And *orare* means "to pray".

13
    Review:

What do these words mean?

beatum
culpa
ideo
precor
omnes
pro
Dominum

If you miss one, look it up, and write it down.

Review Exercises

Translate into Latin:

1. I confess

2. I beseech

3. I confess to almighty God.

4. that I have sinned greatly

5. in thought, word, and deed

6. through my own fault

7. I beseech all the saints

8. and you, brethren

9. to pray for me

10. to the Lord our God

Lesson 19: <u>Misereatur</u>

1
       There are two *misereatur* prayers. The first is spoken by the altar-boy to the priest, and the second is spoken by the priest to everybody. So they are slightly different.

       In the first one, spoken by the altar-boy to the priest, the Latin words for "you" and "your" are in the singular. In the second one, spoken by the priest to everybody, the Latin words for "you" and "your" are in the plural.

2
       Misereatur is an "r-verb". So, like *confiteor* and *precor*, it ends with an "-r".

       Misereatur is in the "may-form". The official name for the "may-form" is the "subjunctive". You may use that term, if you prefer. The subjunctive occurs several times in the words of the Mass.

       Misereatur....Deus means "<u>may</u> God have mercy". When you translate a verb in the subjunctive, you will often want to use the English helper-verb "may".

       The subject of the verb *misereatur* is *Deus*. Usually in Latin the subject comes before the verb. Here it comes later. In English, word-order makes all the difference. In Latin, word-order doesn't matter very much.

       The dictionary-form of *misereatur* is *misereor*, just like *confiteor*. Try to guess what the may-form of *confiteor* would be.

3

Omnipotens means "almighty". You can remember that by thinking of the English word *omnipotent*. The English adjectives *omnipotent* and *almighty* are synonyms. Synonyms are words that have the same meaning.

Omnipotens is an adjective in the nominative singular, and it goes with *Deus*.

What does *omnipotens Deus* mean?

4

Misereatur tui Deus means "May God have mercy on you".

In English we say "have mercy on somebody".
"On" is a preposition. "On you" is a prepositional phrase.

Latin is different. There is no preposition. And the Latin verb *misereor* is actually followed by the genitive case!

Tui is the genitive case of *tu*. Now, even though *tui* is the "of-form" of *tu*, we are still not going to say, "of you". We are going to say "on you", because that is the idiom required by the rules of English.

Say and translate:

Misereatur tui omnipotens Deus.

5
Dimissis peccatis tuis

This phrase is easy to translate, but it is hard to explain. So we won't try to explain it. We'll just play with it.

First, change the word-order to make it more like English:

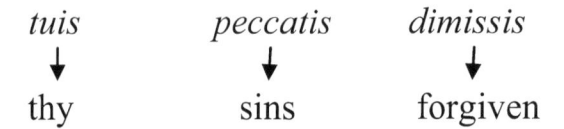

tuis	*peccatis*	*dimissis*
↓	↓	↓
thy	sins	forgiven

All three Latin words are in the ablative plural. And for future reference—a few years from now—this construction is called the "ablative absolute". Meanwhile, this is the only place where an ablative absolute occurs in the words spoken by the altar-boy.

Now, keep the English translation, but restore the original Latin word-order:

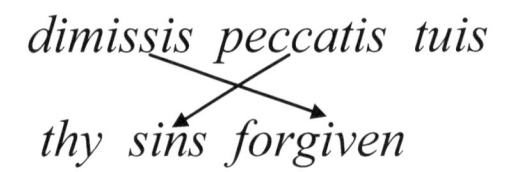

dimissis peccatis tuis
thy sins forgiven

6
If you want to add the English word "with" to your translation, that will be perfectly acceptable. Thus:

<u>with</u> thy sins forgiven

7
Now say and translate:

Misereatur tui omnipotens Deus
et, dimissis peccatis tuis....

8

Perducat te ad vitam aeternam

Perducat is a verb. The subject of *perducat* is "He", referring to "Almighty God".

(Remember that in English we have to say words like "he". In Latin they are often left out, because they are hidden in the ending of the verb.)

Perducat is in the "may-form".

Now, just for a moment, forget about the meaning of *perducat*. We shall translate it (temporarily) as:

"may he verb".

9

.... te ad vitam aeternam

te means "you". *te* is in the accusative case, because it is the direct object of *perducat*. So our temporary translation so far will be:

"may he verb you"

10

.... ad vitam aeternam

What part of speech is *ad*?
What case does *ad* take? (This means: what is the case of any noun that follows *ad*?)
What does *ad* mean?

If you can answer all of those questions, give yourself a pat on the back. If not, look the answers up, and write them down. And write down the page-number where you found them. And give yourself a punch on the nose.

11
    .... vitam aeternam

vitam aeternam is a noun-phrase. It consists of a noun plus an adjective.

    i. The noun is *vita*.

vita means "life", and it is in the accusative singular. It has to be accusative, because it comes after *ad*.
What English word comes from *vita*?

    ii. The adjective is *aeternam*.

aeternam means "everlasting". *aeternam* modifies—or goes with—*vitam*. You can tell that, because they have exactly the same endings.
Think of another English adjective, which sounds like *aeternam*, and happens to be a synonym of "everlasting".
What are *synonyms*?

12
    What does *vitam aeternam* mean?
    What does *ad vitam aeternam* mean?
    What does *te ad vitam aeternam* mean?

13
    Now let's go back to a earlier problem, which we left unsolved. We still have not translated the verb *perducat*. Here is the point that we have now reached:

"May he *perducat* you to everlasting life."
              or
"May he *verb* you to everlasting life."

Your job here is to guess what *perducat* means. Write down your answer.

14

Perducat means "may he lead" or "may he bring".

What is the dictionary form of *perducat*? What does it mean?

We have already seen another verb with nearly the same meaning as *perduco*. What was that verb?

Hint: it ended in *–erunt*.

If you can't think of the answer, look back and find it. And then write down the other verb and the page where it can be found.

And finally, guess the "may-form" of the other verb.

15

The prefix *per-* ....oops! what's a prefix?

A prefix is an extra syllable stuck on the front of a word. For example, in English we have a verb "turn" and another verb "re-turn". The extra syllable "re" is a prefix. Here are a few more examples: *tend* and *pretend,* or *side* and *off-side*. Now think of an example by yourself. Hint: try using *un-* as the prefix.

The prefix *per-* suggests the idea of "all the way to". However, if you will glance at a Missal, you will see that those words are usually not included in the translation.

16

Say out loud and translate:

Perducat te ad vitam aeternam.

17
    Here are the two versions of the *Misereatur*:

Misereatur **tui** omnipotens Deus, et dimissis peccatis **tuis**, perducat **te** ad vitam aeternam.

Misereatur **vestri** omnipotens Deus, et dimissis peccatis **vestris**, perducat **vos** ad vitam aeternam.

    Draw a circle around all the differences. Explain the differences.

    Now translate both versions into English. If you need to look back for help, that's fine. But write down the page numbers.

    Are the English versions the same, or different? Look in your Missal, and see what it says.

18
    <u>Review of the 2nd person singular pronoun: *you*</u>.

    The Latin for "you" is "tu".

    The nominative case is "tu": *Quia <u>tu</u> es, Deus, fortitudo mea*.

    The genitive case is "tui": *Miseratur <u>tui</u> omnipotens Deus*.

    The dative case is "tibi: *Confitebor <u>tibi</u> in cithara*.

    The accusative case is "te": *perducat <u>te</u> ad vitam aeternam*.

    The ablative case is also "te": *plebs tua laetabitur in <u>te</u>.*

    "Running through the cases" is called "declining". When you decline *tu*, you say :
    tu
    tui
    tibi
    te
    te

    How fast can you do that? Now shut your eyes, and decline *tu* again. Faster, please.

    PS: In England they do it in a different order. And in this book we haven't reached the ablative of *tu* yet.

Review Exercises

A. <u>Translate into English</u>:

1. Misereatur

2. Misereatur tui

3. Misereatur tui Deus

4. Misereatur tui omnipotens Deus

5. dimissis peccatis tuis

6. perducat te

7. ad vitam aeternam

B. <u>Translate into Latin</u>:

8. May the Father have mercy on you,

9. and may the Son lead you to eternal life,

10. [with] your sins forgiven.

Lesson 20: <u>Indulgentiam</u>

1

V. Indulgentiam, + absolutionem, et remissionem peccatorum nostrorum tribuat nobis omnipotens et misericors Dominus.

R. Amen

This prayer is one sentence, and it contains some long words. But it is actually quite easy.

2

Start with *tribuat*.

Tribuat is a verb in the may-form. It means *may he grant*.

Now observe: *Dominus* is in the nominative case. Therefore the noun *dominus* is the subject of *tribuat*. And the core-phrase in this long sentence is

tribuat....Dominus

So we don't need the pronoun "he" any longer, because we have a named subject.

The core-phrase *tribuat Dominus* means "may the Lord grant".

Notice that the subject *dominus* here occurs way after the verb *tribuat*. We cannot do things like that in English. In Latin, word-order is more flexible.

3

Tribuat Dominus, May the Lord grant

Now we want to know: May the Lord grant WHAT? And TO WHOM?

The WHAT? is the direct object. It will be a noun-phrase in the accusative case.

The TO WHOM? is the indirect object. It will be a noun or a pronoun in the dative case.

So our sentence will look like this:

May the Lord grant ...... something .... to somebody.

4

We mentioned "indirect objects" on page 54. But we didn't define the term, or give any examples. Let's look at a few examples.

Aedan sent a letter. (Careful! There is no indirect object here yet.)

What is the subject? What is the verb? What is the direct object?

Aedan sent his mother a letter.

What is the indirect object? And here is the same question in different words: What is the "to whom?".

Hey Aedan, shoot me the puck!

What is the indirect object?

5

Here is a useful trick. The indirect object can always be rewritten as a "to-phrase". Like this:

Aedan sent his mother a letter
$\rightarrow$ *Aedan sent a letter <u>to his mother</u>* .

Now you do that trick with the other example:

Hey Aedan, shoot me the puck!

6

Where were we? Oh yes,

Indulgentiam, + absolutionem, et remissionem peccatorum nostrorum tribuat nobis omnipotens et misericors Dominus.

The core-phrase is *tribuat Dominus*. It means "may the Lord grant".
The indirect object is *nobis*. *Nobis* is a pronoun in the dative case. *Nobis* means "to us".
So the core-phrase + the indirect object is: *tribuat nobis Dominus*. And that means "may the Lord grant to us", or simply "may the Lord grant us".   (Yes, sometimes you can skip the word "to".)

7

What about *omnipotens et misericors*?

Omnipotens and *misericors* are two adjectives in the nominative singular. They go with (or "modify") *Dominus*, which is also in the nominative singular.

So we have a noun-phrase *omnipotens et misericors Dominus*. The only word that you might not know there is *misericors*. It means "merciful".

Say and translate:
Omnipotens et misericors Dominus.

8

The core-phrase is *tribuat Dominus*, "may the Lord grant".....

Insert the indirect object, and we get: *tribuat nobis Dominus*, "may the Lord grant us".......

Then add the adjectives, and we get: *tribuat nobis omnipotens et misericors Dominus*:

Translate that, please. (yes, out loud)

9

That leaves the direct object! We have finished everything else.

Actually there are three direct objects. And, as you might expect, they are all in the accusative case.

indulgentiam	=	"pardon" or "indulgence"
absolutionem	=	"absolution"
remissionem	=	"remission" or "forgiveness"

10

Peccatorum nostrorum is in the genitive plural. So it is in the "of-form". And it means "of our sins".

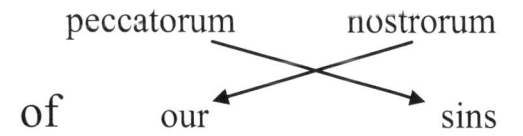

```
       peccatorum      nostrorum
              \       /
               \     /
                \   /
                 \ /
                 / \
   of        our     sins
```

Which Latin word means "sins"? Which Latin word means "our".

11
    We can temporarily revise the word-order of this prayer, to make it look more like English:

Omnipotens et misericors Dominus
tribuat nobis
indulgentiam, absolutionem, et remissionem
peccatorum nostrorum.

12
    And now we can insert a translation in small print. We will begin with the word "may", because that is a requirement of English grammar.

Omnipotens et misericors Dominus
May the almighty and merciful Lord

tribuat nobis
grant [to] us

indulgentiam, absolutionem, et remissionem
pardon, absolution, and remission

peccatorum nostrorum
of sins our.

PS: The word for "our" in Latin usually comes AFTER its noun. For example: *Pater noster,* which means *Our Father*.

Review Exercises

Translate into Latin:

1. may [he] grant

2. may the Lord grant

3. may the Lord grant [to] us

4. almighty and merciful

5. pardon

6. absolution

7. and remission

8. of our sins.

Lesson 21: <u>Deus, to conversus</u>

1

    V: Deus, tu conversus vivificabis nos.
    R: Et plebs tua laetabitur in te.

2

    Deus could be nominative or vocative. But it is followed by a comma. Therefore, it is vocative.
    Deus means "God!", or "O God...."

    What does *Deus, tu* mean?
    PS: When you see a question in this book, you should answer it!

3

    The verb in this sentence is *vivificabis*.
    Vivificabis means "you will give life to". Some Missals use older language and says: "thou...shalt quicken". *Quicken* does <u>not</u> mean "go faster". It means "bring to life".
    Vivificabis and *tu vivificabis* mean the same thing. They should be translated the same way. But *tu vivificabis* is more emphatic.

4

    Vivificabis is in the 2nd person singular (also know as "you"). And it is in the future tense. So *vivificabis* is in the "you will" form.
    If we keep the old-fashioned word *quicken*, then *vivificabis* means "you will quicken".
    Compare *introibo*. What did *introibo* mean?
    What would *vivificabo* mean?
    What would *introibis* mean?

5

    Nos means "us". *Nos* is in the accusative case, because it is the direct object of *vivificabis*.
    Say and translate:
    Deus, tu vivificabis nos.

6

What about *conversus*?

Here is the long answer: *Conversus* is the perfect participle of the deponent verb *convertor*. Okay, forget the long answer.

Conversus is a verb-form, but it behaves like an <u>adjective</u>. *Conversus* goes with *tu*.

However, because the form *conversus* comes from a verb, it is more difficult to translate. We have to say something like

"turning around"
or
"turning back"
or even
"looking back".

You could call these English phrases "verbal adjectives". They are hybrids. Notice that they all have an "-ing".

7

Read and translate these words in the following (wrong) word order:

Deus, conversus tu vivificabis nos.

Write your translation down.

Now restore the word order:
Deus, tu conversus vivificabis nos.

But leave your translation alone. It's fine.

8

The Missal translates *conversus* as a verb. Look and see. That may be the best solution.

Read the translation in the Missal out loud. Now paraphrase that translation into modern English. (If you don't know what "paraphrase" means, guess!)

9

Deus, tu conversus vivificabis nos.

"Oh God, you *adjective* will *verb* us."

Supply a suitable adjective (with "ing"). And then supply a suitable verb.

10

Now do the same job with TWO verbs

"Oh God, you will *verb* and *verb* us."

11

Now let's make this a little bit harder. *Conversus* really means "having turned around", or "after turning around".
Try to work that idea into your translation.

12

We have looked at several different ways to translate one Latin sentence. Think about it for a moment, and then say which way you prefer.

13

Et plebs tua laetabitur in te.

Take a deep breath. Relax. This one is easy.

What does *et* mean? What does *in te* mean? What does *tua* mean? Hint: *altare tuum, tabernacula tua*.

That leaves two words. The words are *plebs* and *laetabitur*.

14

Plebs is a noun. It is feminine, and it is in the nominative singular. *Plebs* is the subject of the verb *laetabitur*.

Plebs means "people".
What does *plebs tua* mean?

In early Latin *plebs* meant "common people". The English adjective *plebeian* means "lower-class", or "vulgar".

At Westpoint—the United States Military Academy—first-year cadets are called "plebes".

15

Laetabitur is an "r-verb". The -bi- tells you that this verb is in the future tense.

Laetabitur means "shall rejoice" or "will rejoice".

Say and translate:

plebs tua

plebs tua laetabitur

et plebs tua laetabitur in te.

16
    Here are three hard problems. You can skip them if you are tired.

i) Do you remember *confitebor*? If not, refer to page 83.

    What did *confitebor* mean?
    What would *laetabor* mean?
    What would *confitebitur* mean?

ii) Why is the fourth Sunday in Lent called *Laetare Sunday*? Look in your Missal for the answer.

iii) Translate this sentence into Latin. (!!!! yoiks)

Thy holy people will praise thee in Sion.

Review Exercises

Translate into Latin:

1. O God, thou

2. having turned around

3. thou shalt give us life

4. and thy people

5. will rejoice

6. in thee.

Lesson 22: <u>Nearly Finished</u>

1

    R: Deus, tu conversus vivificabis nos.
    V: Et plebs tua laetabitur in te.

Look back to Lesson 21 if you need to. Write down some notes, if you need to. Then translate those words into English.

2

    Ostende nobis, Domine, misericordiam tuam.

Domine is the vocative of *Dominus*. We use the vocative to name the person to whom we are speaking. The vocative and the nominative are usually the same form; but here they are different.

Domine means "O Lord".

3

    If you delete a noun in the vocative, you should always be left with a grammatically correct sentence. Here it is:

Ostende nobis misericordiam tuam.

Ostende means "show". Verb in the command-form, aka the imperative. What is the dictionary form of *ostende*?

nobis means "us" or "to us". Pronoun in the dative case. Indirect object of *ostende*.

misericordiam means "mercy". Noun in the accusative case. Direct object of *ostende*.

4

    Read and translate:

    Ostende nobis....

    Ostende nobis misericordiam.

    Ostende nobis misericordiam tuam.

    Ostende nobis, Domine, misericordiam tuam.

5

    Et salutare tuum da nobis.

Da: Verb in the "command-form", aka the imperative. *Da* means "give". The dictionary form is *do*. What does *do* mean? What does *da* mean?

Salutare: Noun in the accusative case. Direct object of *da*. *Salutare* means "salvation". Where have we seen *salutare* before?

You know all the other words in this sentence. So now you can translate

    Et salutare tuum da nobis.

6

    Domine, exaudi orationem meam.

You already know the words *Domine* and *meam*. What do those words mean? What cases are they in?
Exaudi: Verb in the imperative. *Exaudi* means "hear" or "answer".
Orationem: Noun in the accusative. *Orationem* means "prayer".

So now you can translate:
Domine, exaudi orationem meam.

7
Et clamor meus ad te veniat.

The English word *clamor* means "loud shouting". The Latin word *clamor* means "cry".

What does *ad te* mean?

Veniat is a verb in the "may-form". It means "may come". *Veniat* has a subject. The subject is *clamor meus*. So actually

clamor meus veniat

means

May clamor meus *come*

or

Let clamor meus *come.*

Now you can translate

Et clamor meus ad te veniat.

8
Dominus vobiscum

You already know the word *Dominus*. It is in the nominative case, because it is the subject.

Dominus vobiscum means "The Lord be *vobiscum*. We have to add the word "be" in English, even though Latin can leave it out.

9

>If we keep the same word order,
>>*vobis-cum* means "you-with".

Vobis means "you". And *cum* means "with". But Latin reverses the word order, and makes one word out of two.

So what does *vobiscum* mean?

What does *Dominus vobiscum* mean?

10

>*Et cum spiritu tuo.*

Cum is a preposition. *Cum* takes the ablative case. So *spiritu* is a noun in the ablative case.

What familiar noun is *spiritu* the ablative of? Or, to ask the same question in a different way: What is the nominative case of *spiritu*?

What does *tuo* mean?

11
     Here are the last four "VR pairs" all together. Please recite and translate them, one pair at a time.

    Deus, tu conversus vivificabis nos.
        Et plebs tua laetabitur in te.

    Ostende nobis, Domine, misericordiam tuam.
        Et salutare tuum da nobis.

    Domine, exaudi orationem meam.
        Et clamor meus ad te veniat.

    Dominus vobiscum.
        Et cum spiritu tuo.

Review Exercises

Translate into Latin:

1. O Lord

2. Show us, O Lord,

3. thy mercy.

4. And thy salvation

5. give us.

6. hear my prayer

7. and let my cry come to you

8. The Lord [be] with you.

9. And with your spirit.

Lesson 23: Suscipiat Dominus

1

Suscipiat is a verb in the "may-form".

Suscipiat Dominus means "may the Lord accept"

2

What does *Dominus* mean? Is there any word for "the" in Latin?

What does the word *suscipiat* mean by itself? What is the dictionary-form of *suscipiat*? What does the dictionary-form mean?

3

Review:

Latin verbs have an invisible pronoun embedded in their ending. For example:

amas means "you love". And *tu amas* also means "you love".

amat means "he loves", and *Dominus amat* means "the Lord loves".

We don't say, "The Lord HE loves". We just say, "The Lord loves".

Moral of the story: When we have a noun in the nominative case, we skip the embedded pronoun.

Find the pages where we discussed this idea before.

4

        Suscipiat Dominus sacrificium

Sacrificium means "sacrifice".

Sacrificium is a noun in the accusative case. It is the direct object of *suscipiat*.

What does *suscipiat Dominus sacrificium* mean?

5

The rest of this prayer is a series of 3 prepositional phrases.

1. *de* something,
2. *ad* something, and something and
3. *ad* something else.

6

De means "from"

De manibus means "from hands".

What does *de manibus tuis* mean?

7

Read out loud and translate:

Suscipiat Dominus sacrificium de manibus tuis

8

ad laudem et gloriam nominis sui

ad means "to", or "for". ("For" is a new meaning: you have not seen it before.)

laudem et gloriam means "praise and glory". They are both in the accusative case. *Ad* is always followed by the accusative case.

We will skip the dictionary-form of *laudem*. If you are clever, you may be able to guess the dictionary-form of *gloriam*. (Hint: the priest often sings it.)

9

sui means "his".

Now think carefully: what is the 2nd Latin word in the Mass?

If you take that word (the 2nd word in the Mass), and you put it into the "of-form" (aka the "genitive case), you get *nominis*.

What does *nominis sui* mean?

10

Say out loud and translate:

ad laudem et gloriam nominis sui

Write down the correct answer.

11
ad utilitatem quoque nostram

ad means "for"

quoque means "and", or "and also". You can decide which word works best in English here.

utilitatem....nostram means "our benefit", or "our good".

What does *nostram* mean? What case is the phrase *utilitatem nostram* in? How do you know? (If necessary, look back one page.)

What does *utilitatem* mean? What English word comes from *utilitatem*?

ad utilitatem quoque means exactly the same thing as *et ad utilitatem*.

Say and translate:
ad utilitatem quoque nostram

12

totiusque

-que means "and". *–que* is not a word. *–que* is a suffix.

A suffix is a syllable added to the end of a word. Take the English word "amaze", and add a suffix to it, so that you get another word. (What word did you get?)

totiusque has exactly the same meaning as *et totius*.

They both mean

"and of all".

13

Ecclesiae suae sanctae

These words are a noun-phrase in the genitive case.

Ecclesiae suae means "of his Church".

What does *Ecclesiae suae sanctae* mean?

14

Say and translate:

totiusque Ecclesiae suae sanctae

Review Exercises

<u>Translate into Latin:</u>

1. May the Lord accept

2. the sacrifice from your hands

3. for the praise and glory of his name

4. for our benefit also

5. and [the benefit] of all his holy Church.

<u>Try these as well:</u>

6. the Father and the Son (use *et*)

7. the Father and the Son (use *–que*)

8. and of all (use *et*)

Lesson 24: This can't be right!

Here are some sentences in odd English. Although these sentences are not in normal English, please translate them into Latin.

You should be able to find the answers in your mind—in your own Latin memory—even though you might not be sure what the words mean.

Hint: Begin by filling in the words you are sure of.

(PS: If you just cannot do this exercise, you are allowed to look in your Missal. The answers are located just before the Preface, and the Preface is just before the Sanctus.)

[the] Lord [be] you-with!

And with spirit your.

Up, hearts!

We have, to [the] Lord.

Thanks let-us-give to Lord God our.

Worthy and right it-is.

Review Exercises

<u>Translate into Latin:</u>

1. with you

2. with spirit

3. up!

4. hearts

5. we have

6. We have the Lord God.

7. thanks

8. Let us give thanks.

9. I give thanks.

10. It is right.

Lesson 25: Pater Noster

You already know the *Our Father* in both English and Latin. Now we can put the two languages together.

In this exercise please write the meaning of each Latin word in English beneath the word. Use old-fashioned English or modern English, as you prefer. Some of the words have already been done.

You may be surprised to find that there will be differences between your new English translation, and the familiar version that you already know by heart!

Pater noster
Father

Qui es in caelis
Who

Sanctificetur nomen tuum
Hallowed-be

Adveniat regnum tuum
May-come

Fiat voluntas tua
Done-be

sicut in caelo et in terra
as also on

Panem nostrum quotidianum
Bread

Da nobis hodie
today

Et dimitte nobis
forgive

debita nostra
debts

sicut et nos dimittimus
also forgive

debitoribus nostris
debtors

Et ne   nos   inducas in tentationem
not   *lead*

Sed libera nos a malo.

PS
    In caelis and *in caelo* mean the same thing. They both mean *in heaven*. But *caelis* is plural. So you could also translate *in caelis* as "in the heavens".

    Did you find this exercise hard or easy?

    If you found it easy, then look at all the differences between your new English translation, and the version that you memorised when you were little. What is the biggest difference?

    If you found it hard, no problem! The answers are at the end of the book.

Lesson 26: <u>Communion</u>

1

    Pax Domini sit semper vobiscum

There are two words here that you have not seen before. The two new words are

    pax

and

    sit.

2

Pax means "peace".

What does *pax domini* mean?

3

If you know the answer to that question, you can skip this section and go on to #4.

Domini is the "of-form" of *dominus*. *Domini* is the genitive case of *dominus*. And *dominus* means "lord".

Now what does *pax Domini* mean?

4

Sit is the "may-form"—or the subjunctive—of the verb *to be*.

Sit means "may it be".

5

Where have I seen *semper* before?

[Gloria Patri et Filio et Spiritui Sancto, sicut erat in principio et nunc et <u>semper</u> et in saecula saeculorum, Amen.]

So what does *semper* mean?

Look on page 96, if you need to.

6

    What does *vobiscum* mean?

    Look on page 128, if you need to.

7

    Now let's put all the pieces together.

Pax Domini
    the peace of the Lord
sit
    may it be

semper vobiscum
    always you-with.

8

    Oops, that's not very good English. Let's improve the translation:

May the peace of the Lord be always with you.

9

Domine non sum dignus

    Domine is the vocative of *Dominus*. We use the vocative case, in order to name the person to whom we are speaking. Another way of expressing this Latin sentence would be:

    O Domine, non sum dignus

    What does *Domine* mean?
    (If you need help, look on page 125.)

10

    Sum means "I am".

    What does *non sum* mean?

11
    Did you say "not I am"?   If so, please fix your funny English.

12
    Dignus means "worthy".

    What does *non sum dignus* mean?

13
    We have now seen all 3 singular forms of the verb *to be* in the present tense. Please translate the following into Latin:

    I am

    you are

    he, she, or it is

Here are two hints, if you need them. 1) *Quia tu.... Deus fortitudo mea.* 2) *Dignum et justum....*

14
    non sum dignus ut intres

    ut intres means "that thou shouldst enter" or "that you enter"

15
    sub tectum meum

    "under my roof"

    What is the Latin word for "roof"?

16
    sed tantum dic verbo

    "but   only   say   the word"

17

    et sanabitur anima mea

    "and *anima mea* will be healed"

    Try to guess "anima mea". Hint: *anima* means "soul".

18

    Now say the whole prayer out loud; and then translate it into English:

    Domine, non sum dignus,
    ut intres sub tectum meam,
    sed tantum dic verbo,
    et sanabitur anima mea.

19

    Corpus Domini nostri Jesu Christi
    custodiat animam tuam
    in vitam aeternam

There are two words here that you might not recognise. The first is *corpus*, and it means "body".

    corpus = body

The other word is *custodiat*. The dictionary-form is *custodio*. It means "keep" or "preserve". *Custodiat* is in the "may-form", like *tribuat* and *suscipiat*.

    You should now be able to translate the whole prayer into English. The easiest way to start is like this:

May the Body of.....

    Please finish the translation. If you have forgotten anything, turn back as far as you need, and look it up.

Review Exercises

Translate into Latin:

1. The peace of the Lord

2. be ever with you.

3. Lord, I am not worthy

4. that thou shouldst enter under my roof.

5. My soul will be healed.

6. The body of our Lord

7. May the body of our Lord preserve your soul.

8. unto eternal life

27 <u>Blessing</u>

Benedicat vos omnipotens Deus

You know that *vos* means "you".
You know that *omnipotens* means "almighty".
And you know that *Deus* means "God".

Benedicat is a new word. It means "may (he) bless". And in English we can skip the pronoun "he", because we have *Deus* as a subject.

Benedicat is in the "may-form". *Benedicat Deus* means "may God bless". What is the dictionary-form of *benedicat*? What does it mean?

Now read the whole blessing, and translate it into English. You will find it helps, if you start your translation with the word "May":

Benedicat vos omnipotens Deus:
Pater, et Filius, et Spiritus Sanctus.

    And may God bless you for serving Mass.
    You have finished the book. And we have ended in the same place, where we began in Lesson 3: with the Sign of the Cross and the Trinity.

Answers to Review Exercises

Lesson 2, page 16

Another form of *pater* is *patris*.
Another form of *filius* is *filii*.
Another form of *sanctus* is *sancti*.

Patris means "of the Father".
Filii means "of the Son".

Lesson 3, page 22

Cases are the different forms of nouns.
We use the ablative case after *in*.
We use the genitive case to mean *of*.
The English language has a possessive case, eg *John's*.

Lesson 4, page 25

nomen
Pater
Filius
In nomine Patris et Filii

Lesson 5, page 32

A
The nominative of *patris* is *pater*.
The nominative of *Filii* is *Filius*

Spiritūs sanctī OR *sanctī Spiritūs*
(Both answers are right, because word order does not matter.)

B
Pater sanctus
Filius sanctus
Filii sancti
Patris sancti

Lesson 7, page 41

1. you
2. 4 times
3. thou
4. I
5. him
6. them

Lesson 8, page 46

2a: Past tense
2b: Present tense, present tense
2c: Future tense (with a helper verb)

Lesson 9, page 52

1. ad altare
2. ad Deum
3. ad altare Dei
4. introibo
5. introibo ad altare Dei

Lesson 10, page 56

2. laetifico

Lesson 11, page 62

1. nomine
2. sanctus
3. introibo
4. altare
5. Deum
6. juventutem (can also be written *iuventutem*)
7. judica (or *iudica*)
8. discerne
9. causam
10. meam

Lesson 12, page 68

1. Judica me, Deus
2. Discerne causam meam
3. Erue me
4. Erue me ab homine iniquo
5. Erue me de gente non sancta
    or
   Libera me de gente non sancta

Lesson 13, page 76

1. juventutem meam
2. causam meam
3. fortitudo mea
4. Tristis es
5. Tristis introibo
6. Repulisti me
7. Inimicus me affligit
8. dum
9. quia
10. quare

Lesson 14, page 82

1. emitte
2. lucem tuam
3. et veritatem tuam
4. Emitte lucem tuam et veritatem tuam.
5. Ipsa me deduxerunt.
6. in montem sanctum tuum
7. et in tabernacula tua
8. Ipsa me deduxērunt et adduxērunt.

Lesson 15, page 89

1. introibo
2. confitebor tibi
3. in cithara
4. Deus, Deus meus
5. Quare tristis es, anima mea?
6. Et quare conturbas me?
7. quia tu es, Deus, fortitudo mea
8. Quare me repulisti?
9. Inimicus me affligit.
10. ad Deum, qui laetificat juventutem meam.

Lesson 16, page 93

1. Spera
2. Spera in Deo
3. Confitebor tibi
4. Confitebor illi
5. salutare vultūs mei
6. Spiritūs Sancti
7. spiritūs mei
8. Emitte lucem tuam et veritatem tuam
9. ad altare
10. ad Deum

Lesson 17, page 98

1. Gloria Patri
2. et Filio et Spiritui Sancto
3. sicut erat in principio
4. et nunc et semper
5. Adjutorium nostrum
6. in nomine Domini
7. Adjutorium nostrum in nomine Domini.
8. qui fecit
9. qui fecit caelum et terram
10. Dominus fecit terram.

Lesson 18, page 105

1. confiteor
2. precor
3. Confiteor Deo omnipotenti
4. quia peccavi nimis
5. cogitatione, verbo, et opere
6. meā culpā
7. Precor omnes sanctos
8. et vos, fratres
9. orare pro me
10. ad Dominum Deum nostrum

Lesson 19, page 113

1. May he have mercy.
2. May he have mercy on you.
3. May God have mercy on you.
4. May almighty God have mercy on you.
5. your sins having been forgiven
    OR
   with your sins forgiven
6. may he lead you
7. to eternal life

8. Misereatur tui Pater,
9. et perducat te Filius ad vitam aeternam,
10. dimissis peccatis tuis.

Lesson 20, page 119

1. tribuat
2. tribuat Dominus
3. Dominus tribuat nobis (Any word-order will be fine.)
4. omnipotens et misericors
5. indulgentiam
6. absolutionem
7. et remissionem
8. peccatorum nostrorum

Lesson 21, page 124

Thy holy people will praise thee in Sion
Plebs tua sancta confitebitur tibi in Sion.

1. Deus, tu
2. conversus
3. vivificabis nos
4. et plebs tua
5. laetabitur
6. in te

Lesson 22, page 130

1. Domine
2. Ostende nobis, Domine
3. misericordiam tuam
4. et salutare tuum
5. da nobis
6. exaudi orationem meam
7. et clamor meus ad te veniat
8. Dominus vobiscum.
9. Et cum spiritu tuo.

Lesson 23, page 136

1. Suscipiat Dominus
2. sacrificium de manibus tuis
3. ad laudem et gloriam nominis sui
4. ad utilitatem quoque nostram
5. totiusque Ecclesiae suae sanctae

6. Pater et Filius
7. Pater Filiusque
8. et totius

Lesson 24, page 138

1. vobiscum
2. cum spiritu
3. sursum
4. corda
5. habemus
6. Habemus Dominum Deum
7. gratias
8. Gratias agamus
9. Gratias ago.
10. Justum est.*

* Some Latin Missals do not use the letter "j". Instead, they use "i" for both "i" and "j". They write *iustum* insetad of *justum*. Both spellings are common. In this book we have used "j", because it is easier. Just remember that "j" has a "y" sound.

Lesson 25

Pater noster
Father our

Qui es in caelis
Who are in heaven

Sanctificetur nomen tuum
Hallowed-be name your

Adveniat regnum tuum
May-come kingdom your

Fiat voluntas tua
Done-be will your

sicut in caelo et in terra
as in heaven also on earth

Panem nostrum quotidianum
Bread our daily

Da nobis hodie
Give us today

Et dimitte nobis
And forgive us

debita nostra
debts our

sicut et nos dimittimus
as also we forgive

debitoribus nostris
debtors our

Et ne nos inducas in tentationem
And not us lead into temptation

Sed libera nos a malo.
But deliver us from evil.

Answers to Review Exercises

Lesson 26, page 146

1. Pax Domini
2. sit semper vobiscum.
3. Domine, non sum dignus
4. ut intres sub tectum meum.
5. Sanabitur anima mea
6. Corpus Domini nostri
7. Corpus Dominis nostri custodiat animam tuam
8. in vitam aeternam.

My Latin Vocabulary

Words are listed alphabetically. They are listed under their dictionary-form, even though that form might not occur in the text. Some—but not all—other forms are also given.

a, ab + ablative (The "b" is used before a vowel.)
    from
absolutio, *acc* absolutionem
    absolving, absolution
aeternus
    eternal, everlasting
ad + accusative
    to, toward, at
adduco, *3rd pers plu past* adduxērunt
    lead, bring

adhuc
    still
adjutorium
    help
advenio, *may-form* adveniat
    come
aeternus
    eternal
affligo
    afflict, harass

altare
    altar
amen
    Amen
anima
    soul
apostolus, *dat plu* apostolis
    apostle
archangelus, *dat* archangelo
    archangel

baptista, *dat* baptistae
　　baptist, baptiser
beatus
　　blessed
benedico, *may-form* benedicat
　　bless
caelum, *abl sing* caelo, *abl plu* caelis
　　heaven, sky
causa, *acc* causam
　　cause, case

cogitatio, *abl* cogitatione
　　thought
confiteor, *fut* confitebor
　　confess, praise, give praise to
cithara, *abl* citharā
　　harp, lute
clamor
　　cry
conturbo
　　disturb, trouble, disquiet

conversus
　　turning around, after turning around
cor, *plu* corda
　　heart
corpus
　　body
culpa, *abl* culpā
　　fault
cum + abl
　　with

custodio, *may-form* custodiat
　　keep, guard
de + ablative
　　from
debitor, *dat plu* debitoribus
　　debtor, sinner
debitum, *plu* debita
　　debt, sin, trespass
deduco, *3rd pers plu past* deduxērunt
　　guide, lead

Deus, *gen* Dei, *acc* Deum
> God

dico, *imperative* dic
> say

dignus, *neut* dignum
> worthy

dimissus
> forgiven

dimitto, *imperative* dimitte
> forgive, release

discerno, *imperative* discerne
> distinguish

do, *imperative* da
> give

dolosus, *abl* doloso
> guileful, tricky

Dominus, *gen* Domini
> Lord

dum
> while

ecclesia, *gen* ecclesiae
> church

ego, *acc* me, *abl* me
> I, me

emitto, *imperative* emitte
> send forth, send out

eram, eras, erat
> I was, you were, he was

eruo, *imperative* erue
> rescue, save, deliver

et
> and

exaudio, *imperative* exaudi
> hear, answer (a prayer)

facio, *3rd pers sing past* fecit
> make

fio, *may-form* fiat
> be done

filius, *gen* filii, *dat* filio
> son

fortudo
    strength, power
frater, *plu* fratres
    brother
gens, *abl* gente
    nation, people, race
gloria
    glory
gratias
    thanks

gratias agamus
    let us give thanks
habeo, *1st pers plu* habemus
    have
hodie
    today, this day
homo, *abl* homine
    man
ideo
    therefore, and therefore

ille, *dat* illi
    he
in + ablative
    in, on
in + accusative
    to, unto, onto, into
incedo
    walk in, go in
induco
    lead

indulgentia
    forgiveness, indulgence
inimicus
    enemy
iniquus, *abl* iniquo
    wicked, evil
introeo, *fut* introibo
    enter, go in
intro (*ut intres = that thou shouldst enter*)
    enter

ipse, *neut plu* ipsa
    it, he, *plu* they
Joannes, *dat* Joanni
    John
judico, *imperative* judica
    judge
justus, *neut* justum
    right, just
juventus, *acc* juventutem
    youth, boyhood

laetifico
    gladden, make joyful
laetor (deponent verb), *3rd pers sing fut* laetabitur
    rejoice
laus, *acc* laudem
    praise
libero, *imperative* libera
    deliver, free
lux, *acc* lucem
    light

malum, *abl sing* malo
    evil
manus, *abl plu* manibus
    hand
Maria
    Mary
maximus, *fem abl sing* maximā
    very great, most grievous
meus, *fem nom* mea
    my

Michaël, *dat* Michaëli, *acc* Michaëlem
    Michael
misereor + gen, *may-form* misereatur
    have mercy on
misericordia, *acc* misericordiam
    mercy, kindly heart
misericors
    merciful
mons, *acc* montem
    mountain, hill, mount

nimis
> greatly, a lot

nomen, *gen* nominis, *abl* nomine
> name

ne
> not

non
> not

nos, *dat* nobis
> we, us

noster, *fem* nostra, *neut* nostrum
> our

omnipotens, *dat* omnipotenti
> almighty

omnis, *dat plu* omnibus
> all

opus, *abl* opere
> deed

oratio, *acc* orationem
> prayer

oro, *infin* orare, *imperative plu* orate
> pray

ostendo, *imperative* ostende
> show

panis, *acc* panem
> bread

pater, *gen* patris, *dat* patri
> father

pax
> peace

peccatum, *acc plu* peccata
> sin

pecco, *past tense* peccavi
> sin

perduco, *may-form* perducat
> bring, lead

Petrus, *dat* Petro
> Peter

Paulus, *dat* Paulo
> Paul

plebs
> people

precor
> beseech, beg

pro + abl
> for

quare
> why

qui
> who

-que (suffix)
> and

quia
> because

quoniam
> because

quoque
> also

quotidianus, *acc* quotidianum
> daily

regnum
> kingdom

remissio, *acc* remissionem
> remission

repello, *2nd pers sing past* repulisti
> reject, push away, drive away

sacrificium
> sacrifice

salutare
> salvation

sanctifico
> hallow, keep holy

sanctus, *gen* sancti, *dat sing* sancto, *dat plu* sanctis
> holy

sanctus (noun)
> saint

saeculum, *plu* saecula, *gen plu* saeculorum
> age, world

sano (*sanabitur = will be healed*)
> heal

semper
> ever, always

sicut
> as

sit (*may-form of* est)
> may it be

spero, *imperative* spera
> hope

sub
> beneath

sursum
> up, lift up!

spiritus, *gen* spiritūs, *dat* spiritui
> spirit

sum, es, est
> I am, you are, he is

suscipio, *may-form* suscipiat
> accept, receive

tabernaculum, *plu* tabernacula
> tabernacle, dwelling place, tent

tantum
> only

tectum
> roof

tentatio, *acc* tentationem
> temptation

terra, *acc* terram
> earth

totus, *gen* totius
> all, whole

tribuo, *may-form* tribuat
> grant

tristis
> sad

tu, tui, tibi, te, te
> you (singular)

tuus
> your, thy

ut
> that

utilitas, *acc* utilitatem
    benefit

venio, *may-form* veniat
    come

verbum, *abl* verbo (*say the word = dic verbo*)
    word

veritas, *acc* veritatem
    truth

virgo, *dat* virgini
    virgin

vita, *acc* vitam
    life

vivifico, *2ⁿᵈ pers sing fut* vivificabis
    give life to, make alive

vobiscum
    with you

voluntas
    will

vos, *gen* vestri, *dat and abl* vobis
    you (plural)

vultus, *gen* vultūs
    face

Printed in Great Britain
by Amazon